Dedicati

Zora Arkus-Duntov
1909-1996

He joined Chevrolet in 1953, the same year the Corvette was introduced. With a rich background in engineering and racing, Zora Arkus-Duntov called the first Corvette a "sheep in wolf's clothing" and made it his personal mission to transform it into a world-class performer. By 1957, Corvettes were ruling racetracks around the country, attaining the high-performance reputation many say is the reason for its unique forty-year reign as *the* American sports car.

With respect and appreciation, this *Illustrated Corvette Buyer's Guide* is dedicated to the memory of Zora.

Corvette

Michael Antonick

MBI Publishing Company

This edition published in 2002 by MBI Publishing Company, Galtier Plaza, Suite 200, 380 Jackson Street, St. Paul, MN 55101-3885 USA

MBI Publishing Company books are also available at discounts in bulk quantity for industrial or sales-promotional use. For details write to Special Sales Manager at Motorbooks International Wholesalers & Distributors, Galtier Plaza, Suite 200, 380 Jackson Street, St. Paul, MN 55101-3885 USA.

Library of Congress Cataloging-in-Publication Data Available

ISBN 0-7603-1485-3

On the front cover: 1997 Corvette. *Jerry Heasley*

On the back cover: 1956 Corvette. *Jerry Heasley*

Printed in the United States

CREDITS AND ACKNOWLEDGEMENTS

My thanks to everyone who contributed in any way to the information and photos contained in this book. Special thanks to:

Noland Adams, Dan Aldridge, John Amgwert, Bob Applegate, Pat Baker, Jane Barthelme, Sanford Block, Becky Bodnar, Michele Boling, Kent Brooks, Barry Brown, Dale Brown, David Burroughs, Steve Dangremond, Dr. M. F. Dobbins, Jim Downing, Bob Eckles, Sam Folz, Steve Guckenberg, Dick Guldstrand, Dr. Joe Haase, John Hibbert, Mike Hunt, John Hyland, Rick Johnson, Alan Kaplan, Ed Kenney, Paul Kitchen, Gary Konner, Jim Krughoff, Gary Lisk, Bill Locke, Bob Lojewski, Bob McDorman, Terry Michaelis, Chip Miller, Bill Mock, Bill Munzer, Jeffrey Painter, Brian Pearce, John Poloney, Donna Sims, Jon Solt, Wes Raynal, Bill Rhodes, Doug Robinson, Jeffrey Smith, Mark & Dixie Smith, Lou Vitale, Jerry Wadsworth, Jerry Weichers, Don Williams, and Kathy Williams.

All Corvettes Are Red–James Schefter, Simon & Schuster
Chevrolet by the Numbers–Alan L. Colvin, Robert Bentley, Inc.
Corvette! America's Star Spangled Sports Car–Karl Ludvigsen/Automobile Quarterly
Corvette Restoration & Technical Guide, Vols 1 & 2–Noland Adams, Automobile Quarterly
Corvette! The Sensuous American–Michael Bruce Associates, Inc.
The Corvette Black Book–Michael Bruce Associates, Inc.
Vette Vues–James Prather
Vette Vues Fact Book 1963-1967 & 1968-1972–Dr. M. F. Dobbins
1953-1972 Corvette Pocket Spec Guide–National Corvette Restorers Society

Bob McDorman Chevrolet
Callaway Engineering
Chevrolet Motor Division of General Motors
Mercury-Marine
Mid America Designs
National Corvette Restorers Society

Mike Antonick

TABLE OF CONTENTS

INTRODUCTION

The Corvette is a uniquely American phenomenon. Speak of Corvettes and someone within hearing range will join in as an expert. And if you find a person who hasn't owned a Corvette, he'll tell you he plans to own one, has always wanted one, has an uncle with five or a neighbor in the middle of a "body off" restoration. If Chevrolets are as American as apple pie, surely the Corvette must be the pie à la mode.

The Corvette has developed quite a following and reputation. Part of the reputation is the widespread belief in Corvettes as great investments. Owning a Corvette is a sure way to beat depreciation. Is it true?

A qualified yes. Historically, many Corvettes have held their value well or appreciated significantly. But there are exceptions.

Purchased new, a Corvette depreciates as any other car. Some salesmen would have you believe a new Corvette depreciates less than comparably priced American makes. Some Corvette models have, some haven't.

Anyone considering a new Corvette purchase who plans to keep it a few years or less should forget the investment angle. Operating expenses for the Corvette will be similar to other cars in the same price range. Corvette depreciation might well be less, but that will likely be offset by higher fuel, maintenance, and insurance costs.

But what if you're planning to keep a new Corvette for a long time? Better yet, what if you're planning to get an older model? That's different.

Something interesting happens to nearly all Corvettes as they age. Depreciation stops and appreciation begins.

Mention "appreciation" and the accountant in the crowd says cars are not good investments if one looks carefully at the real rate-of-return. True enough, but cars aren't stocks and bonds. You can't drive a treasury note. Cars are instruments of utility and pleasure. Very expensive instruments, by the way. The cost for operating even an average-priced new car today over a three-year period can easily exceed $10,000 annually. Fuel prices have spiked during shortages, but the lion's share is always depreciation.

Shrewd Corvette owners have learned they can eliminate depreciation from the operating cost equation and replace it with some appreciation, which in some cases is enough to offset other costs. In effect, free driving.

Over the long run, would a smart Corvette purchase beat a solid investment in stocks, bonds, or treasury notes? Don't bet on it. Would a smart Corvette purchase beat most other automotive purchases? Yes, especially if the Corvette has aged beyond its depreciation cycle and become "collectible."

You've heard stories of tremendous profits (and losses) made buying and selling Corvettes. Many factors influence the market for collectible Corvettes. Following the 1987 stock market crash, for example, people with disposable funds to invest faced a dilemma. The stock market's future seemed uncertain and interest rates were modest, so for about two years money poured into "hard" assets like coins, art, and collectible automobiles. Stir a little media hype into this stew, and some Corvettes went on one wild roller-coaster price ride. In early 1987, the market for a nice 1967 435-hp "big block" roadster was $25,000-$35,000. By mid-1989, some of these Corvettes had tacked $100,000 onto their values!

Like most markets that go nuts, this one "corrected." Prices started slumping in 1989 and by 1991, that $130,000 1967 Corvette's value was cut in half.

But there's another way to look at it. Throw out the peaks and valleys and a price appreciation graph for collectible Corvettes would show very respectable appreciation over time. A price analysis for an earlier edition of this book calculated twenty-percent annual appreciation between 1975 and 1986 for several Corvette models. That's enough to warm any CPA's heart.

For shock value, consider the five 1963 Corvette Grand Sports built by Chevrolet to challenge Carrol Shelby's Cobra. Grand Sports changed hands for a few thousand dollars in the sixties. Today it's $1 million and climbing. Strong six-figure prices are paid for special models like 1967's L88. Yet many 1967 Corvettes are modestly priced. These examples illustrate that the Corvette market runs nearly as wide a gamut as any of the so-called exotics.

The real world has thousands of older Corvettes available for purchase. Corvettes worth owning are never cheap, but I think even at today's appreciated prices, many are bargains. Over the years I've observed that a really superb older Corvette was worth about the same as the current new model. It was true in 1962, 1972, 1982, and 1992. I think it will continue to be true.

Demand is the reason. More and more people recognize what these older Corvettes were . . . and are. They want one. Why is the Corvette perceived as so desirable?

Construction of the car is one reason. For years Corvettes were criticized by magazine writers for a chassis that was overbuilt and unnecessarily heavy. It was a valid gripe because a lighter chassis with less-robust components would have been more fuel efficient. But from a prospective buyer's viewpoint, the rugged construction of older Corvettes is purely advantageous.

Chevrolet mated a fiberglass body to that strong chassis. Fiberglass doesn't rust, ever. But this doesn't mean rust is never a Corvette problem. Corvette frames rust, some so badly they have to be replaced.

The marriage of fiberglass body to metal frame meant the Corvette could never be of unit-body (body and frame welded together as a unit) construction. Unit-body versus separate body/chassis construction means little to a new car buyer, but body/chassis construction is a restorer's dream come true. After some disconnects and removal of body bolts, six average men can lift the entire body off a Corvette chassis in an afternoon (the post-1984 models are a bit more complicated). Corvettes are built the way they are because of the fiberglass-to-metal-frame marriage, but Chevy engineers couldn't have created a more ideal car for restorers if that had been their top priority.

Another factor in the Corvette value story is what sort of car it is. The Corvette was born into Detroit's high performance era. In many ways it was the star of the show. Even as the industry was forced to shift gears from performance to economy, safety, and pollution control, the Corvette remained a performer relative to its competitors. As the industry came to grips with its new challenges, the Corvette led the way back to high performance, combined with improved comfort, convenience, and extraordinary handling.

When I wrote the first edition of this book in 1983, I pointed out that Corvette buyers had quite a range of cars from which to select. There were the first-generation Corvettes, the solid rear axle models built from 1953 to 1962. The second-generation "mid-year" Corvettes were the popular 1963 to 1967 models. And the third generation included 1968 through 1982. As I write this fourth edition, added to the mix is the complete fourth-generation range of 1984 through 1996, and the fifth-generation ("C5" in Chevy-speak) ushered in by the all-new 1997. Selecting from the five generations is no easy task and many Corvette enthusiasts solve the problem by owning more than one. That's up to you, but I do want to explain some elements in the development of the Corvette "world" as it exists today.

The contemporary sports car phenomenon is said to have started in this country when our servicemen returned from Europe with cars like the MG. But more important to the Corvette story is that when the servicemen returned to their wives and wives-to-be, they created the post World War II baby boom. The Corvette came along at the tail end of the boom and the two, the Corvette and the babies, grew up together. This was a golden era of auto production, an era when designs changed rapidly and kids sneaked around dealerships before introduction dates hoping for a glimpse of new models. For many of these young people, the Corvette represented the ultimate car dream.

This combination of events, Detroit's golden years, postwar babies, the Corvette's emergence as the performance dream car, is unique in auto history. No matter what era a young car-lover grew up in, there has always been some great car of the day to dream of. But cars usually get better as the years roll on. By the time those young people could afford the dream car of their youth, it no longer stacked up very well compared to newer offerings.

Not true for the Corvette; and this factor is a big one in the Corvette story. Boomers who would've done about anything to have a 1961, or a 1963 split-window coupe, or a 1967 roadster, grew up. When it was time to buy the car they'd dreamed of, the very same car looked and performed better than most then available in new-car show rooms.

A personal example: I had just graduated from high school when the 1963 was introduced. I walked into the local Chevy dealership cold. Thanks to the secrecy of the era, I hadn't seen a single photo of the new Corvettes. Friends told me the new "vettes" were slick, but I didn't pay much attention. Corvettes had never appealed to me all that much.

The first 1963 I saw, a Daytona Blue, fuel-injected split window coupe, stunned me. I walked around it in awe for an hour. No new car has ever done what that one did to me. My first Corvette came five years later, a well-worn 1963 convertible. Years later when I could afford a new car, guess what I bought. An immaculate 1963 coupe. Daytona blue. Fuel injected. Having been around Corvettes for a while, I assure you this is not a unique story.

What counts most is that Corvettes are great cars. If they weren't, the mystique, baby boom, fiberglass bodies . . . all of it wouldn't matter if it turned out Corvettes weren't worth owning.

Of course it's no longer true that a brand-new Corvette can't perform up to the level of older models. But that period when it was true led to the development of a tremendous aftermarket business for Corvette parts and related merchandise. It is far easier to maintain or restore any model Corvette today than it was years ago. In the early seventies, I once bought a Corvette just so I could switch its nice passenger seat with my worn-out driver seat. Now there are countless suppliers offering a range of products to satisfy almost any need.

The parts availability in the Corvette aftermarket greatly reduces financial risk for a first-time buyer. A Corvette in your driveway may not impress the neighbors as much as a Lampredi V-12 Ferrari, but the risk factors aren't in the same league. Pick a Ferrari with a sour motor and the repair bills could cost more than you pay for a gem of a Corvette . . . the whole car!

Don't think you can't make a mistake buying a Corvette. The consequences of making an error just aren't likely to be as painful as with other makes. Provided you don't buy a bogus Corvette, paying too much is like paying too much for good real estate. Eventually you'll be okay. It just takes longer.

There's no need to go through the pain of a poor purchase and that's what this book is all about. It's written with the assumption that you're not a Corvette expert and its purpose is twofold: to help you decide which Corvette model is best for you, and to help you select a good example.

Like any major purchase decision, you should research the subject thoroughly. Interest in Corvettes has led to many excellent Corvette books. There are also monthly magazines loaded with articles, and ads for Corvettes and parts that will give you a good feel for the market.

Where should your search for the right car begin? The common first choice is a local newspaper. For someone starting to look, it isn't the best choice. Nor is a monthly Corvette magazine. Anyone just beginning should expose himself to a lot of examples. Looking at cars advertised in the media takes too much time. Even the selection at a dealer specializing in Corvettes may not be adequate. Many people who try to find their first Corvette without much exposure either jump into the purchase too quickly and get the wrong car, or they get so frustrated looking they give up.

I recommend going to a Corvette show. Other marques have shows, but none compare to Corvettes in this arena. There are hundreds held each year, ranging from small local events to major ones that draw 30,000 people. Shows are sometimes built around a concours competition, but the real attractions are the parts vendors and the buying and selling of Corvettes between individuals. Some shows conduct all-Corvette auctions. These are great for a first-time buyer as learning experiences, but I wouldn't recommend purchasing at an auction until you're comfortable with your expertise level.

Major shows include Knoxville, Tennessee, in mid-March; Bloomington, Illinois, in June; and Corvettes at Carlisle, Pennsylvania, in August. I love the big swap meet held several times a year at the Los Angeles County Fairgrounds in Pomona, but Corvettes are a small part of that event's appeal. Local Corvette enthusiasts can tell you which area shows are worthwhile. In Ohio, we have a one-day swap meet at the Lima fairgrounds in March, and the Bob McDorman Chevrolet show in Canal Winchester in September that are personal favorites. I've not made it to the Spearfish show in the Black Hills of South Dakota, but friends tell me it is a gem. The National Corvette Restorer's Society moves its annual convention to different locations each year, but its Cypress Gardens event in Florida is always in January and is always excellent. Believe me, this list just scratches the surface.

Go to just one good Corvette show and you'll see more Corvettes in a day than years of newspaper searching will yield.

Should you buy a Corvette at a show? Possibly, but the best Corvettes, especially older ones, are often not found at shows, or auctions, nor advertised in newspapers or magazines. They're sold by word of mouth. When someone has a topnotch Corvette for sale, the word spreads.

Finding a car by word of mouth is easier said than done for someone just entering the market. But it's not as hard as it sounds. Contacts you make with a local Corvette club, regardless of whether you join, can pay off. So can the right word placed with a few people at your local Chevy dealership.

Once you've gone to a few shows and have a clearer idea of what you're after and the right questions to ask, you should definitely search monthly magazines like *Corvette Fever*, *Cars & Parts*, *Hemmings Motor News*, *Vette* and *Vette Vues*, as well as dealers. The car you call about might not be the right one, but the conversation could lead to it. Expose yourself.

More important than where you find a Corvette is the scrutiny you give it before buying. Taking along a knowledgeable Corvette buff really pays off. What you have to avoid at all costs is unknowingly buying a bogus Corvette. Bogus? There's that word again.

Simply put, a bogus Corvette is not what it appears. It's a 1964 coupe that's been altered to look like a more valuable 1963 split window. Or it's a 1968 with a disguised 1976 Camaro engine. Or it's four wrecks pieced together into one. The caliber of the seller can be an indication, but not necessarily. He may have been stuck by someone else and is trying to unload.

A bogus Corvette is a fake, and there are lots of them. For example, real fuel-injected Corvettes of the variety built between 1957 and 1965 are rare and valuable. There are probably twice as many fuel-injected Corvettes in existence today than GM ever built.

Is originality such a big deal? So what if an engine or a few components have worn out? Doesn't a demolished Corvette deserve to be brought back to life? If everything works, what's the difference? The difference is in the Corvette's value. Originality is tremendously important to Corvette enthusiasts. It is to any auto enthusiast group, but Corvette buffs take it to extremes.

I'm not sure why. Part of it may be a backlash to all the modifications done to Corvettes during the hot rod era. A lot of Corvettes have been abused. If an older Corvette survived with all components intact, it's a good indication that it's been reasonably well treated. Also, Corvettes have been a favorite of thieves for years. Most often they were stripped, the parts winding up on cars from one end of the country to the other.

There's something unsettling about all this to Corvette enthusiasts, which makes them insist that a Corvette be as close as possible to the way it left the factory. It's a serious consideration and greatly affects a Corvette's value.

Most ads for older Corvettes contain a statement like "all numbers match." Many people who advertise this way don't know themselves what numbers they're referring to, but figure they'd better say they're correct since everybody else does. *Illustrated Corvette Buyer's Guide* will explain the "numbers" so that you'll be able to determine with reasonable assurance that the Corvette you're considering for purchase is what it's represented to be.

In some ways, this emphasis on numbers has run amok. As an owner, what you do with your own car is largely your own business. There are laws regarding safety and emissions, of course, but an owner has every right to change colors, interiors, components, and the like. It is the representation of an automobile as something it is not that can constitute fraud. Misrepresentation usually doesn't include the bit of embellishment engaged in by most sellers. It is something like converting a base-engine 1967 into a 435-horsepower "original" with phony papers to prove it. Be careful in your representations, and in interpreting those of others.

Many people looking for a used car take their "mechanic" along. If you're after a Corvette and your mechanic isn't a Corvette specialist, his usefulness to you is limited. He can tell you some things about the car's general operating condition, but this is only part of what you need to know. Take along someone who can also help you determine the Corvette's originality.

Does it matter if a Corvette is a different color than originally painted by the factory? Yes, especially if it's a 1963 or later model, because the correct color is coded into trim plates on the car. As a general rule, a wrong-color repaint devalues a Corvette by the amount it would cost to correct it.

Body damage is another area of importance. Some people place great value on a Corvette that has had minimal bodywork. I'm one of them. It's not easy to find exactly what you want in an older Corvette—and find it with no body damage history to boot—but I'd sacrifice a few other things for a straight body. Corvettes with extensive damage, particularly front end, never seem to look right again. This is especially true of 1963 and later models with hidden headlights.

One of the first things to do when inspecting a Corvette is to get it on a big level parking lot and walk around it awhile. If it's been whacked, it'll show up in bad panel alignments, cocked bumpers . . . a kind of disheveled look.

But Corvettes weren't flawlessly built by General Motors. Paint repairs at the factory were not unusual, especially at the St. Louis facility. And some body flaws occur naturally with age. To an untrained eye, some things that look like signs of a crash aren't. This is another good reason to get to a show and view as many Corvettes as possible. You'll learn that stress-cracking of paint due to flexing of the fiberglass body is normal. But if you look at enough examples of the model you're interested in, you'll also know that the cracks occur in predictable areas. Finding one with cracks where they don't normally occur is a sign of trouble.

Though the main body shell of 1953-1982 Corvettes looks like a single piece of fiberglass, it isn't. It is made up of many panels, much like a metal car, that are bonded together. At the point the panels bond, a groove is created. The factory filled and sanded these grooves before painting, but it is common for seams to separate slightly or for the filler material to shrink a little. Barely visible seam lines on a Corvette with a few years' use are to be expected and don't reduce its value at all, unless it's being presented and priced as a concours specimen.

If a series of little dimples around the seams are seen, watch out. The dimples are probably filled holes created by screws or rivets that temporarily held the panels in position during a repair. Investigate thoroughly. Possibly it was just a minor scrape that only popped the panels loose. Or the damage may have been serious enough to require panel replacements.

After fighting all the problems associated with filling, sanding, and finishing fiberglass body seams, Chevrolet engineers eliminated visible seams starting with the 1984 Corvette model by hiding them behind rub strips, casting larger panels, or somehow just designing around them. So visible surface problems with these models can't be passed off as seam flaws.

I shouldn't overemphasize the repair aspect. You can find Corvettes with absolutely no body damage, but you may rule out some perfectly fine examples in the process. The important thing is to remove as much mystery as possible before buying. Nothing's worse than buying what you thought was a jewel, only to discover the following morning the nose has been replaced from the wheelwells forward. I've done it. Twice.

As a matter of courtesy, don't demand to drive a Corvette that's for sale unless you have some interest in it. One of the bad things about being on the selling side is the number of joy-riders who show up with no intention of purchasing. If all stacks up correctly and you've found a genuine candidate, by all means give it a thorough shakedown. Don't abuse it. The owner will likely want to ride along and I've heard of some who refused to sell to someone who acted like the village idiot on the test drive.

Start by giving the Corvette the same scrutiny you would any used car. Ailments often show up as sounds, so listen carefully. If equipped with manual transmission, don't "speed shift," but do shift briskly through all gears. Downshift through the gears at reasonable rpm. Double-clutching the downshifts is fine once you own it, but not when you're test driving, as this could hide marginal synchronizers.

Speaking of transmissions, there's been quite a shift in customer preference over the years. In the mid-sixties, manual transmissions made up about 90 percent of Corvette sales. Today, it's only about 20 percent. For newer models, dealers will tell you a manual transmission is tougher to sell and thus worth less. That's good news for diehards like me who will own nothing but a manual.

I can't describe to you how the model Corvette you want should feel and sound when you drive it. You'll have to develop the experience yourself. I'll tell you this: I've driven a few 1963 Corvettes that were breathtakingly exciting. Exaggerating very little, I've also driven some that felt and sounded like dump trucks—breathtaking in their own bizarre way, but not worth owning. Many Corvettes have been terribly abused. Others have been subjected to amateur restorations. There is a world of difference in used Corvettes and in the way they drive.

Obviously, the ideal used Corvette is a well-maintained, low-mileage original purchased from its own owner with a documented history from the date of purchase. They're around but scarce and expensive.

Don't get too hung up on miles. The nicest driving older Corvette I've experienced is one I owned for seventeen years, a 1967 with real miles in the teens. The next best was a friend's nearly identical 1967 with well over 100,000 miles. An abused Corvette can be shot after a few thousand miles. A cared-for Corvette will drive well indefinitely.

I think the single biggest mistake a first-time Corvette buyer can make is to pay too much for a Corvette that needs lots of work. Someone unfamiliar with the Corvette parts aftermarket will underestimate refurbishing costs every time. Unless you're itching to do your own complete restoration, my advice is to pay the additional price for a solid, complete, and correct car. It's been my observation for years that many excellent Corvettes don't sell for what they're worth, but fixer-uppers sell for too much.

The next chapters of *Illustrated Corvette Buyer's Guide* deal with individual Corvette models and will help you narrow your choices before the search begins. As you read these chapters, another of the Corvette's great virtues becomes apparent. Thanks to a variety of engines and options, Corvettes can be about any kind of car you want, from air-conditioned highway cruisers to race cars. And everything in between.

INVESTMENT RATING

✪✪✪✪✪   The best investments. Already expensive, but continued high appreciation can be expected. The finest examples are most often sold or traded between Corvette enthusiasts without advertising.

✪✪✪✪   Excellent investments. More affordable than five-star-rated Corvettes, but still expensive with high appreciation anticipated. These are often sold or traded among enthusiasts, but they can also be located at Corvette shows and meets, and are often advertised in Corvette-only publications.

✪✪✪   Very good investments. These are less expensive than four- or five-star-rated Corvettes and will appreciate at lower rates, but are still solid values. Because of their lower cost and a correspondingly larger market, cars in this category are particularly attractive to first-time buyers.

✪✪   Good investments. These are Corvettes which are too new to be in the appreciation cycle, or older models which haven't developed a strong appreciation history. There are possible "sleepers" in this category, which could develop into tomorrow's three- or four-star models.

✪   Marginal investments. Corvettes don't belong in this category unless they've been seriously damaged, substantially modified, or have had major components (i.e., engine) changed.

The star rating system above requires interpretation for Corvettes. With just a few exceptions, annual Corvette production has always far exceeded that of "exotic" sports cars. Corvettes are not scarce, but some Corvettes with special equipment are.

Some of the chapters that follow group several Corvette model years. The groups are star-rated according to their overall strength and popularity. Within each group—each year for that matter—there are Corvettes which both exceed and fall short of the group rating and the more significant ones are given separate ratings where appropriate. For example, Chapter Six covers 1963 and 1964 models, which are very similar, and as a group the two years merit a four-star rating. However, many of these models with desirable options are strong five-star investments. The ratings always require some judgment and common sense application by the prospective buyer.

The one-star rating has not been given to any group because it is a condition rating reserved for problem cars. Any Corvette in any category could be one-star rated. Conversely, very special Corvettes exist in each group which deserve five stars regardless of the group's rating.

After model and equipment, the single most important factor in determining a Corvette's value is its originality. Corvette enthusiasts believe that the ideal Corvettes are those in the condition they were in when built. This concept places great value on highly documented, original cars. Restored Corvettes can be nearly as valuable, provided they've been restored properly to factory specs and haven't been "over" restored. Corvettes worked over by GM Design Staff or Engineering for executives or shows are obviously very desirable, but those customized or modified by individuals, while interesting in their own right, shouldn't be a part of anyone's investment strategy.

CHAPTER 1
1953 CORVETTE

Serial Nos. E53F001001 - E53F001300

Life began for the Corvette in 1951. The initial seed was planted by Harley Earl, the legendary creator of GM's Art and Color Section, which was the predecessor of auto industry styling departments around the world.

Like many great ideas, the Corvette was almost an accident. From 1949 to 1961, General Motors operated its famous Motorama shows, lavish showcases for presentation of each year's new offerings plus a few "dream" cars to pull the crowds in.

In 1951, Earl commissioned a young stylist, Bob McLean, to draw up a two-seater "sports car" for the 1953 Motorama. McLean created the Corvette, Chevy Chief Engineer Ed Cole saw and loved it; and the rest is history.

But it wasn't a smooth history, at least not early on. Cole begged for and got permission to bring the Corvette into the Chevrolet camp and to display it as a running dream car in the 1953 Motorama. If public response justified it, consideration would be given to putting a derivative into production.

Cole decided instead to build the Motorama Corvette as a genuine preproduction prototype. The Corvette went from styling clay model to running prototype in seven months, surely a record of some sort. Cole was gambling that he would get permission to put the Corvette into production and he wanted to be ready. The Corvette was finished in time, barely, for the January kickoff of the 1953 Motorama at the Waldorf Astoria in New York City.

Cole had guessed correctly. The Corvette was a smashing crowd success and Cole got the permission he'd anticipated to rush the Corvette into production.

Rush is hardly the adequate description of the Corvette's blazing journey from idea to reality. In June 1952, it was a clay model. In January 1953, it was a running preproduction prototype. By the end of 1953, Chevrolet managed to introduce the car as a 1953 model and to build 300 units!

The 1953 is the rarest of all Corvette years. About 200 of the 300 built are still known to exist, but the first two off the line have never been accounted for. Officially, they were engineering test vehicles and were destroyed, but no witnesses or documentation has ever surfaced. Find one of these and you'll have found one of the most valuable cars in existence.

All 1953 Corvettes were polo white with sportsman red interiors and had black canvas convertible tops. All were pretty much hand-built in Flint, Michigan, in the back of the customer delivery garage, an old building on Van Slyke Avenue. Chevrolet sensed tremendous demand for the Corvette and readied a plant in St. Louis to build nearly a thousand per month starting with the 1954 model.

On June 30, 1953, the first Corvette was driven off the assembly line in Flint, Michigan. Officially, the first and second Corvettes built were destroyed as test vehicles, but neither a witness nor documentation has ever surfaced. Enthusiasts still dream today of finding Corvette serial number one. Whoever does will have found the most valuable Corvette ever. Chevrolet photo.

The original Motorama Corvette shown here was remarkably similar to the production version that followed. The Chevrolet script above the grille and the air scoops on the front fenders ahead of the windshield were deleted from the production cars. The side body trim was also changed. The photo showing the Chevrolet sedan behind the Motorama Corvette illustrates that the Corvette, with a wheelbase of 102 inches, was not a small automobile. Chevrolet photos.

Visually, the 1953 is a virtual twin to the 1954 and 1955 Corvettes. But because of its scarcity, its hand-built characteristics in the humble Flint facility, and most of all because it started it all, the 1953 is in a category by itself when it comes to ownership.

Contrary to popular belief, 1953 Corvettes are available. The days of finding one in an unknowing farmer's barn for $800 (if those days ever existed) passed twenty years ago. But if you have the financial means, you can buy one. Expect to pay at least double, perhaps triple, the price of a 1954 in comparable condition.

Anyone serious about purchasing a 1953 should plan to join the National Corvette Restorers Society (NCRS) and to attend some of their events. The NCRS is dedicated to the restoration and preservation of 1953 through 1972 Corvettes. In its earlier days, the NCRS limited its membership to owners of 1953 through 1962 models, the so-called classics, and the organization is still top-heavy with these members. Most of the good 1953's are owned by NCRS members, which means attending their events will allow you to view early Corvettes and get firsthand information of those for sale. Joining the NCRS is excellent advice for someone searching for any 1972 or older model.

They may look alike, but the 1953 was not a 1954. In fact, because of the evolutionary way they were hand-produced, an early 1953 was a lot different than a late 1953. So not only do you need to know the differences between the two years, you should also master the 1953 model running changes.

Things unique to the 1953 model included a black oilcloth window storage bag, a black canvas top, special valve cover, one-piece carburetor connecting linkage and a smaller trunk mat. Short exhaust extensions were used on all 1953's and early 1954's, then were extended to eliminate a tendency of early Corvettes to suck exhaust fumes into the cockpit when a vent window was open.

All 1953 and 1954 Corvettes used a Blue Flame six-cylinder engine, a tweaked version of a motor that had been in the Chevrolet stable for years, but the engines installed in the first two Corvette years have different serial coding and some internal running changes.

Very early 1953 models left the factory with Chevy Bel Air "dome" wheel covers before the Corvette covers arrived. The Corvette wheel cover for the rest of 1953 through 1955 was essentially the same design except that a few vendor prototype caps (maybe a hundred) got mixed in with 1953 production. The difference was that the rare caps had the spinner ornaments mounted perpendicular to the center bow-tie emblem. The rest were parallel. The spinners themselves were plated brass forgings at first, then zinc die castings.

Chevrolet didn't offer any 1953 Corvettes with wire wheels, but some dealers added them, hence the "My uncle bought it new and it came with . . ." dilemma. The same is true for hardtops.

When you get right down to it, there's very little leeway in what a 1953 should or shouldn't have. Though listed as options, every 1953 had a radio and heater. All had whitewalls. None had tinted glass, air conditioning, power steering or power brakes. There were no color and trim plates, but it didn't matter. Every 1953 was painted and trimmed to match the Motorama car . . . polo white exterior with sportsman red interior. Period.

With every other Corvette model year, the buyer has some choice of colors and options to weigh into the purchase decision. With the 1953, originality and condition are the value factors.

If you're considering a 1953, it's important to take special note of any missing parts. Some engine components were shared with the passenger car version of the engine. But others, like the valve cover, were unique to the Corvette. The 1953 Corvette valve cover was a highly modified passenger car type (front section flattened to clear hood), which bolted to the head with two studs attached to the top of the rocker arm assembly. Nineteen fifty-three Corvette valve cover decals were also unique. The decals had the words Blue Flame on the passenger side, and Special on the driver side. There's also a lightning bolt decal on the driver side of the cover.

Body parts like the grille, grille oval, bumpers, taillights and especially the side window frames, are expensive to find and purchase. Make a careful list of what parts the car you're interested in needs, and get an idea of their cost before closing the deal. What at first appeared to be an excellent buy may be washed out by the steep cost of parts for the first Corvette series.

Can the 1953 be a good investment? Definitely. The one thing keeping most Corvettes out of the mega-buck collector category is that, compared to foreign exotics, a lot of Corvettes were built and a lot survive thanks to the fiberglass body and generally rugged construction. But production of 300 cars over thirty years ago is low by any measure. The mere scarcity of the 1953 Corvette will keep its appreciation strong.

Is the 1953 a practical year to own? Aside from its value and the special constraints that imposes, definitely yes again. The 1953 does suffer from some problems that nearly sank the entire Corvette boat right after launch — things like a leaky top, less-than-breathtaking performance from its six-cylinder/Powerglide combination and finicky side-mounted carbs — but over the years it has proven to be very durable and generally trouble-free. As an everyday driver, most people would opt for a 1956 or later. A 1954 looks the same as a 1953 to most people at a fraction of the initial cost. But as an investment, the 1953 stands alone.

1953 Corvette

BASE ENGINE

Type:	Chevrolet ohv inline 6
Bore x stroke, inches:	3.56x3.96
Displacement, inches:	235.5
Compression ratio:	8.0:1
Carburetion:	Three Carter single-throats
Horsepower:	150 @ 4200
Distributor:	Single point breaker
Other engines offered:	None

CHASSIS AND DRIVETRAIN

Clutch:	n/a
Transmission:	Two-speed automatic
Front suspension:	Coil springs, tube-type shock absorbers, stabilizer bar
Rear suspension:	Leaf springs, tube-type shock absorbers, rigid axle
Axle ratio:	3.55:1
Frame:	Steel box sections, welded

GENERAL:

Wheelbase, inches:	102
Track, front, inches:	57.0
rear, inches:	58.8
Brakes:	Drum
Tire size, front and rear:	6.70-15
Wheels:	Steel
Body material:	Fiberglass
Assembly plant:	Flint, Michigan

Shortly after the Corvette was introduced in 1953, Chrysler engineers borrowed one from a dealer and photographed it extensively. The photos are valuable to restorers today because they show a very early Corvette completely untouched. These exterior views show ill-fitting panels (note hood), short exhaust tips common to all 1953's and the rare hubcaps with spinners perpendicular to the bow-tie emblem. Chrysler photos.

1953 Corvette Colors/Options		
Color Code	Body Color	Soft Top Color
None	Polo White	Black
INTERIOR COLOR: Red		
Order #	Item Description	Sticker Price
2934	Base Corvette Convertible	$3498.00
101A	Heater	91.40
101B	Signal Seeking AM Radio	145.15

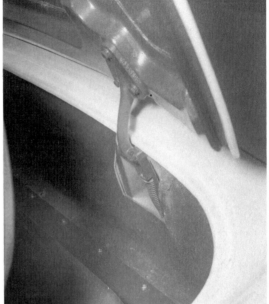

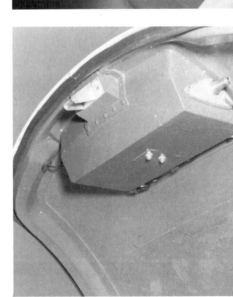

These photos from the Chrysler series show the roughness which was characteristic of early Corvette production. Most restorers today feel it is wrong to correct the roughness for cosmetic appearance. Early Corvettes that have been "over-restored" are usually less valuable than those restored to a state typical of factory build. Chrysler photos.

The side windows of the 1953 Corvette were plastic and had to be removed for storage in black oilcloth bags in the trunk. The soft top folded manually into a storage compartment behind the seats. These features were consistent with European sports cars of the period, but didn't find favor among the country club set "chosen" by Chevrolet to buy the 1953 Corvettes. Chrysler photos.

All 1953 Corvettes had Powerglide automatic transmissions with an unusual floor-mounted selector lever. Some criticized the instrument panel of the first generation of Corvettes for the central placement of engine-monitoring instruments, a shortcoming not corrected until the 1958 model. But to its credit, even the 1953 Corvette came with complete instrumentation including tachometer, oil pressure, battery, water temperature and fuel gauges, and a clock. Chrysler photo.

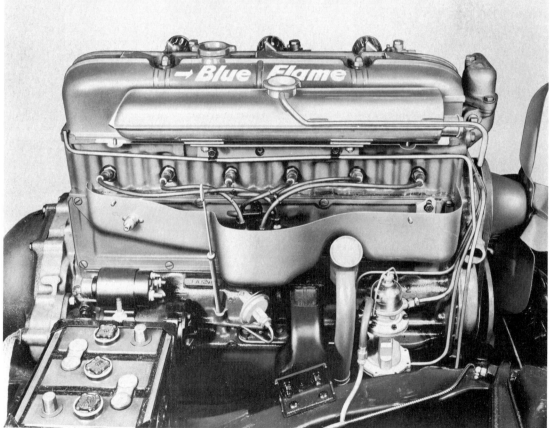

It may not have been exotic, but the Blue Flame six-cylinder engine installed in the first Corvette generation was certainly durable. This
engine, a modified version of one that had been in Chevrolet's stable for
years, required side-draft carburetors and a modified valve cover to
clear the Corvette's low hood. Chrysler and Chevrolet photos.

In the euphoria surrounding the introduction of the Corvette, Chevrolet had visions of producing an entire family of vehicles based on the Corvette, including a station wagon and sport coupe. Disappointing sales canceled those projects and almost canceled the Corvette itself. Chevrolet photo.

(1955)

Serial Nos. 1954: E54S001001 - E54S004640
1955: VE55S001001 - VE55S001700*
(*no "V" prefix for six-cylinder 1955 models)

As planned, Chevrolet shifted production of the Corvette from Flint, Michigan, to a newly prepared facility in St. Louis, Missouri, for the 1954 model. As the 1953 was being mostly hand-built in Flint, tooling designed for higher volume was phased in. For 1954, Chevrolet was all set to roll with the Corvette. The planned 10,000-plus production for 1954 was small compared to GM's other car lines, but still a far cry from the 300 Corvettes made in Flint during the first year.

Chevrolet was ready, but the public wasn't. More accurately, the public had changed its mind. In a classic marketing misfire right up there with the Edsel, Chevrolet had decided to sell its 300 1953 Corvettes to special customers of its choosing, well-heeled status people. This highly discriminating policy would never fly today, but Chevy reasoned then that if high rollers owned the first Corvettes, there'd be a sort of image ruboff.

The problem was that the Corvette rubbed the country club set the wrong way. Remember, the Corvette wasn't cheap. It was a few dollars more than a Cadillac and double a bare-bones Chevy coupe. For Caddy dollars, these folks expected their Corvettes to be two-seat powderpuffs. Imagine their surprise the first time they tried to roll the windows down. They didn't roll down, they unbolted and stored in the trunk. And they leaked, as did the top.

Maybe marketing the Corvette directly to the sports car crowd wouldn't have worked either. Regardless, by the time Chevy was rarin' to go in St. Louis, the market had vanished.

Of the only 3,640 1954 Corvettes built in St. Louis, over 1,100 remained unsold at year's end. Faced with this, Chevrolet slashed 1955 Corvette production to the bone—a mere 700 cars. In so doing, it created the second scarcest model year Corvette.

The Corvette was in real trouble and Chevrolet knew it. By 1954, the problems were clear, but solving them would take some time. In the meantime, Chevy had to resort to the expedient.

One obvious need was for some colors. The white/red combination, which continued to dominate, and a new pennant blue/shoreline beige package accounted for ninety-five percent of 1954 production. A beautiful red/red combination crept in for about three percent. A few black/red cars were also definitely built, but no others have been absolutely confirmed. Some enthusiasts maintain that metallic green and metallic bronze were used in 1954 and cite memos

This photo shows 1954 models in the holding yard outside the new Corvette plant in St. Louis. The plant was designed to produce at least 10,000 Corvettes annually, but only 3,640 were built in 1954 and many of those were unsold at year's end. The Corvette was in trouble. Chevrolet photo.

from paint suppliers to GM as evidence. But no color/trim tags were attached to 1954 or 1955 models, so positive confirmation isn't possible. Since original colors were not color coded to individual cars, some enthusiasts today accept a paint change to another correct color as not particularly sinful.

All the 1954 models had the Powerglide automatic transmission and the six-cylinder Blue Flame engine. Horsepower during 1954 production was increased from 150 to 155. All 1954 models had the 6-volt electrical system common to the 1953. A 1954 engine looked much like a 1953, but there were differences. The serial numbers were different, and the valve cover was different. Where the 1953 Corvette cover attached with two central studs, the 1954 type attached with four bolts around the outside lip. The 1954 Corvette valve cover decals had Blue Flame and 150 reading from the passenger car side, and the 1954 decal lettering was larger than that of the 1953.

To alleviate complaints about power, Chevrolet wedged its hot new V-8 into the Corvette in 1955 and made a manual transmission available later in the year. Most 1955's were V-8-powered but a handful of sixes were built. Interestingly, the V-8's got 12-volt electrical systems, but the six-cylinder models got the old 6-volt electrics. Nobody has ever found a six-cylinder 1955 with anything but a Powerglide transmission. Also, six-cylinder 1955's did not have the frame relief (unique to the 1955) required for V-8 fuel pump clearance.

The six-cylinder engine and Powerglide automatic transmission installed in all 1954 and a few 1955 Corvettes remained the same as in 1953 except for subtle differences. Internally, a camshaft modification during 1954 production increased engine horsepower from 150 to 155. Photos by Bill Locke during the restoration of his 1954 model.

Robust chassis construction of the Corvette is evident in this photo of Bill Locke's 1954. Note the different-style valve cover used on 1954 and 1955 six-cylinder models. The individual bullet air cleaners were used on all Corvettes through serial number E54S003906. Later six-cylinders had an integrated dual-pot apparatus. Bill Locke photo.

The interior of 1954 and 1955 models remained similar to the 1953. Differences included the addition of Conelrad national defense markings to the radio face and a change from two interior hood releases to one early in 1954 production. Tonneau cover snaps are often seen on Corvettes of this period but they were owner additions, since Chevrolet has never offered a tonneau cover option for the Corvette. Author photo.

1954 Corvette Colors/Options

Color Code	Body Color	Soft Top Color
None	Polo White	Beige
None	Pennant Blue	Beige
None	Sportsman Red	Beige
None	Black	Beige

INTERIOR COLORS: Red, Beige

Order #	Item Description	Sticker Price
2934	Base Corvette Convertible	2774.00
100Q	Directional Signal, Polo White	16.75
100R	Directional Signal, Pennant Blue	16.75
101A	Heater	91.40
102A	Signal Seeking AM Radio	145.15
290B	Whitewall Tires, 6.70x15	26.90
313M	Powerglide Automatic Transmission	178.35
420A	Parking Brake Alarm	5.65
421A	Courtesy Light	4.05
422A	Windshield Washer	11.85

1955 Corvette Colors/Options

Color Code	Body Color	Soft Top Color
None	Polo White	White-Beige
None	Harvest Gold	Dark Green
None	Gypsy Red	Beige
None	Corvette Copper	White
None	Pennant Blue	Beige

INTERIOR COLORS: Red, Yellow, Light Beige, Dark Beige

Order #	Item Description	Sticker Price
2934-6	Base Corvette Convertible—6 Cylinder	2774.00
2934-8	Base Corvette Convertible—8 Cylinder	2909.00
100Q	Directional Signal, Polo White	16.75
100R	Directional Signal, Pennant Blue	16.75
101A	Heater	91.40
102A	Signal Seeking AM Radio	145.15
290B	Whitewall Tires, 6.70x15	26.90
313M/N	Powerglide Automatic Transmission	178.35
420A	Parking Brake Alarm	5.65
421A	Courtesy Light	4.05
422A	Windshield Washer	11.85

Corvette buffs argue about exterior colors for 1955 and the picture is even more confusing than 1954. Chevrolet definitely added a Corvette copper with beige interior and a harvest gold (really a yellow) with green and yellow interior. Repeat, green and yellow. GM was willing to try anything!

A red exterior was again available in 1955 but it was combined with a light beige interior instead of red as before. The soft top of the 1954 was canvas like the 1953 except that 1954's were tan. In 1955, soft tops were both canvas and vinyl. And new top colors appeared including white and dark green. Air conditioning, power windows and power steering were not available.

As investments, both the 1954 and 1955 Corvettes have been excellent. Because of the lower number built, and the tendency to abuse the V-8 engine package, good 1955's are much harder to find and are considerably more valuable. Though the Blue Flame six-cylinder was very durable, the Chevrolet V-8 is surely one of history's great motors. It was instrumental in the Corvette's later success, and installed in a 1955 yielded a quick, responsive package combined with the Corvette's original body style. It's a very desirable automobile.

On the other hand, the 1954 model offers the prospective owner the chance to own a genuine classic Corvette for a relatively modest cost, due to the quantity built and the uncommonly high survival rate.

Speaking of survival, you may be wondering how the Corvette managed to survive 1955 when a facility designed to pump out 10,000 cars made a paltry 700. There *was* some corporate ego at stake since Ford introduced its highly successful Thunderbird in 1955; but history tends to give credit for the Corvette's survival to two men: Ed Cole and Zora Arkus-Duntov.

Cole simply never wavered in his love of the Corvette and his belief that it was good for Chevrolet, General Motors and America. He wouldn't take no for an answer.

Duntov came to Chevrolet in 1953 at the age of forty-three after a career mostly in Europe as an engineer and racer. He wasn't hired to transform the Corvette, but he did. He sensed immediately that the Corvette's very life hinged on making it do what it looked like it should. In a word, he made it *go*.

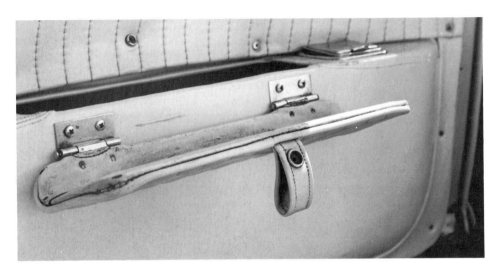

All 1953-55 Corvettes had this handy flip-up armrest cover, which exposed a large storage bin inside the inner door. Author photo.

The 1955 Corvette was a near duplicate of the previous two models, but performance was enhanced by the addition of the V-8 engine and manual transmission. Chevrolet also added several new colors to enhance sales. Despite these efforts, a mere 700 1955 Corvettes were built. Author photo.

The first Corvettes were designed around the six-cylinder engine, so it was necessary for engineers to create a relief in the frame to clear the fuel pump of the V-8. The few 1955's uncovered with six-cylinder engines do not have the relief. Author photo.

1954-1955 Corvette

BASE ENGINE

Type: . . . . .Chevrolet ohv inline 6
Bore x stroke, inches: 3.56x3.96
Displacement, inches: 235.5
Compression ratio: 8.0:1
Carburetion: . . . . .Three Carter single-throats
Horsepower: 150, 155*
Distributor: .Single point breaker
Other engines offered:...*In 1954, only the 6-cylinder was used. Horsepower increased during the year from 150 to 155. In 1955, both the six and a V-8 were considered ''base'' engines. All but a few 1955 Corvettes had the V-8 engine.

CHASSIS AND DRIVETRAIN

Clutch: .Single dry-plate (1955)

Transmission:...Two-speed automatic (standard 1954, optional 1955). Three-speed manual standard in 1955.
Front suspension:...Coil springs, tube-type shock absorbers, stabilizer bar
Rear suspension:...Leaf springs, tube-type shock absorbers, rigid axle
Axle ratio: 3.55:1
Frame: . . . . .Steel box sections, welded

GENERAL:

Wheelbase, inches: 102
Track, front, inches: 57.0
rear, inches: 58.8
Brakes: . . . . .Drum
Tire size, front and rear: 6.70-15
Wheels: . . . . .Steel
Body material: . . . . .Fiberglass
Assembly plant: . . . . .St. Louis, Missouri

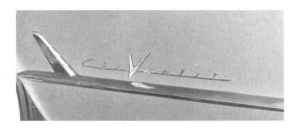

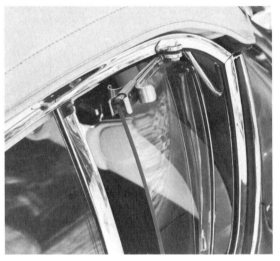

The 1955 Corvette with V-8 engine was identified by a gold "V" incorporated into the Chevrolet side script. The vent window closure clip was used on all 1955 models and late 1954's. Author photos.

The most distinctive feature of 1953 through 1955 Corvettes was the beautifully detailed "fence mask" headlight stone guard. Protection offered by the bumpers of early Corvettes was negligible. Author photo.

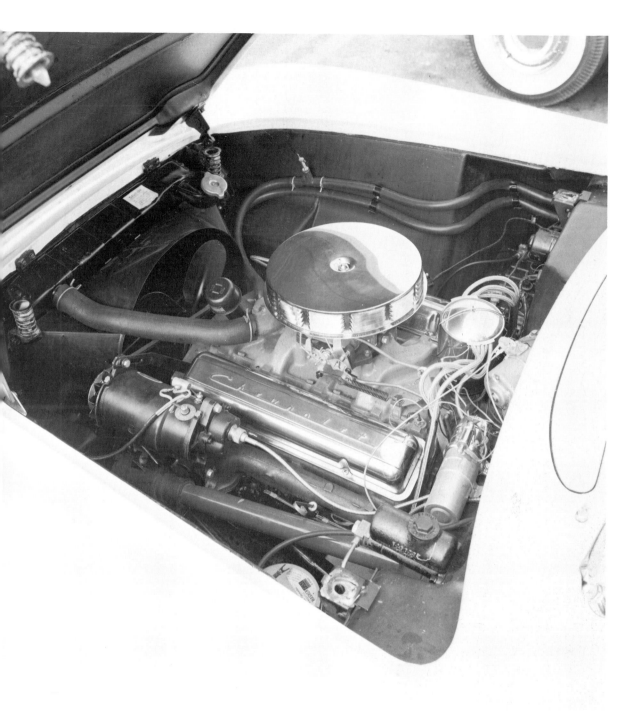

Although only 700 1955 Corvettes were sold, the installation of the V-8 engine signaled the start of the Corvette's transformation into a true high-performance sports car. Good examples of 1955 Corvettes are hard to find because of the low number built and because the V-8 invited abuse. These are excellent investment choices. Chevrolet photo.

Serial Nos. 1956: E56S001001 - E56S004467
1957: E57S100001 - E57S106339

The Corvette was born in 1953 but it grew up in 1956. Chevrolet learned the hard way that as an American car company building an American sports car for American consumption, it was on uncharted ground. Foreign sports cars got away with four- and six-cylinder engines, so what was wrong with putting a Blue Flame six in the Corvette? Foreign sports cars had leaky tops and side curtains instead of windows, so why not the Corvette?

What Chevrolet hadn't realized was that the Corvette was an American sports car, not a foreign one. It would have to cultivate and define its own market. To do so, it would have to be exciting both to look at and to drive. In 1956, Chevrolet started the ball rolling in incredible fashion.

The body for the 1956-57 Corvette was extensively redesigned. The chassis and dash were carryovers from the previous year, but the fiberglass was all new . . . and gorgeous. In one of the styling coups of all time, Chevy's stylists created a masterpiece. These Corvettes were lithe, sculptured works of automotive art, devoid almost entirely of the unnecessary frills and accouterments so common to the era. Other than fake air scoops atop the front fenders, scoops planned to be functional up to the last minute, there was nothing on these cars that didn't belong.

In the first three years of Corvette production, Chevrolet gave the impression that it was confused itself about what the Corvette was and where it was going. Cars were painted colors that officially didn't exist, colors listed as available weren't, 6- and 12-volt electrical systems were used during the same year . . . all of this makes for great conversations and arguments thirty years later among enthusiasts, but it was hardly the kind of organized effort you'd expect from the largest auto producer in the world. But in 1956, Chevrolet got its Corvette act together.

The creature comfort failings of the early Corvettes were corrected. The soft tops fit better, a power unit for raising and lowering the top became optional, a snug factory hardtop was offered and, best of all, the windows were real glass and rolled down. Even power assists for the windows could be ordered.

Six exterior colors were available in 1956 and there's little argument about their use. The V-8 265-cubic-inch engine was the only displacement used, but carburetor and camshaft options yielded horsepower ratings of 225 and 240 in addition to the base 210. A three-speed manual transmission became standard equipment with the Powerglide automatic optional. For the first time in Corvette production, optional differential ratios could be selected.

The styling of the 1956 and 1957 Corvettes was virtually identical and is still considered a masterpiece of sports car design. In all of Corvette history, those two models were the most responsible for charting the Corvette's destiny. Author photos.

The transformation the Corvette went through from 1953 to 1957 was almost unbelievable. As introduced in 1953 with six-cylinder engine and automatic transmission, it had no racing credentials. By 1957, it was almost unbeatable. These photos show the SR-2 (Sebring Racer), one of two built by Chevrolet specifically for racing. Dick Thompson is shown at Marlboro Motor Raceway carrying the checkered flag after he won the C modified and Formula Three event. He set a course record the same day and ultimately went on to win the SCCA championship for Class B production in his 1957 Corvette. Both SR-2 racers are in private hands today. Chevrolet photos.

In 1956, Chevrolet was starting to brew its performance potion. The engines were hot, the optional ones having dual four-barrel carburetion and dual point distributors. The 240-horsepower 1956 Corvette was a far cry from the Blue Flame 150-horsepower model. The 1956 Corvette set the automotive world right on its ear. In three short years, Chevrolet had transformed the Corvette from a cute little car in a nebulous market slot into one of the great sports cars of all time. Then it made it better in 1957.

The two years were lookalikes. From the outside about the only indicator was the rearview mirror visible through the windshield; the 1956 adjusted with a thumbscrew, the 1957 required a wrench. The colors were all the same except that silver was added to the 1957 choices.

What happened to the 1957 Corvette to make the year so special was the addition of two options, fuel injection and four-speed transmission. This was the icing that eliminated every trace of doubt about the Corvette's performance credibility and about Chevrolet's intentions.

Displacement of the V-8 was increased to 283 cubic inches in the 1957 Corvette, and the strongest version of the fuel-injected motor developed 283 horsepower, a number-matching feat that Chevrolet's advertising group made sure no one overlooked. Engines of this strength and other "off-the-shelf" performance items made available in 1956 and 1957 meant that Corvettes in near race form could be purchased right off the show room floor.

Corvettes with the V-8 went racing a little in 1955 with little success. They tried again in 1956 with considerable success. In 1957, they cleaned up. Dick Thompson and Gaston Audrey blew out the competition at the twelve-hour Sebring race in March 1957, for a class victory. Earlier in the year on the Daytona sand, Corvettes places first, second and third in both the flying mile and acceleration runs. To cap it off, Thompson won the 1957 Sports Car Club of America (SCCA) championship for class B production cars in his Corvette.

All of this heritage adds up to two Corvette years that are very desirable. The 1957, because of the justified hoopla surrounding the introduction of fuel injection and four-speed transmissions, commands the higher prices. But only 1,040 of the 6,339 1957's built were equipped with fuel injection. A few fuel-injection units made it onto early cars, but most appeared after serial number E57S102000, the 2,000th 1957 made.

The four-speed transmission became available on May 1, 1957, which approximately equates to 1957 serial number E57S103750, the 3,750th built.

Chevrolet built 3,467 1956 models, less than in 1954. The 1956 is thus quite rare since only in 1953 and 1955 were fewer built. And the 1956 was a rip-snorter, a car that tended to wind up on drag strips and racetracks. Its survival rate is much lower than earlier models.

Both the 1956 and 1957 models ride somewhat harshly. Handling was excellent for its day, but feels dated now. Many owners insist on using original-style tires for appearance, but these are terrible in cornering ability by today's standards. Neither year had power steering, brakes or air conditioning available. Both models are fairly noisy and loose-feeling and the seating support leaves something to be desired for cross-country jaunts. But for short blasts, they're unbeatable. They deliver spine-chilling performance wrapped in a stylish design that still turns every head within blocks.

Parts unique to the 1956 and 1957 models, things like taillights and bumpers, are relatively rare and expensive. Be sure to consider the cost of replacing missing parts for any Corvette of this vintage you're interested in buying.

The 1956 Corvette had a dual four-barrel carburetor package available, but it was the introduction of fuel injection and four-speed transmission in 1957 that really made the motoring world take notice. All 1956 and 1957 Corvettes are excellent investments, but the 1957 with the fuel injection and four-speed transmission options is particularly sought after. Author photos.

The massive grille teeth date the 1956 and 1957 Corvettes to the era, but the single headlight treatment and flowing body forms contribute to an overall design that many feel is the best of the pre-Sting Ray models. Author photo.

The hubcap shown was introduced in 1956 and was used through early 1958. A similar hubcap was used through the end of 1962 production but the later units had holes added to simulate brake-cooling slots. The non-hole version shown is more rare. Author photo.

1956 Corvette Colors/Options

Color Code	Body Color	Soft Top Color
None	Onyx Black	Black/White
None	Aztec Copper	Beige/White
None	Cascade Green	White/Beige
None	Arctic Blue	White/Beige
None	Venetian Red	White/Beige
None	Polo White	Black/White

INTERIOR COLORS: Red, Beige

Order #	Item Description	Sticker Price
2934	Base Corvette Convertible	2900.00
101	Heater	115.00
102	Signal Seeking AM Radio	185.00
107	Parking Brake Signal	5.00
108	Courtesy Lights	8.00
109	Windshield Washer	11.00
290	Whitewall Tires, 6.70x15	30.00
313	Powerglide Automatic Transmission	175.00
419	Auxiliary Hardtop	200.00
426	Electric Power Windows	60.00
449	Special High-Lift Camshaft	175.00
469	Dual Four Barrel Carburetor Equipment	160.00
473	Hydraulic Folding Top Mechanism	100.00

1957 Corvette Colors/Options

Color Code	Body Color	Soft Top Color
None	Onyx Black	Black/White/Beige
None	Aztec Copper	Beige/White
None	Cascade Green	Black/White/Beige
None	Arctic Blue	Black/White/Beige
None	Venetian Red	Black/White/Beige
None	Polo White	Black/White/Beige
None	Inca Silver	Black/White

INTERIOR COLORS: Red, Beige

Order #	Item Description	Sticker Price
2934	Base Corvette Convertible	3176.32
101	Heater	110.00
102	Signal Seeking AM Radio	185.00
107	Parking Brake Alarm	5.00
108	Courtesy Lights	8.00
109	Windshield Washer	11.00
276	5-15x5.5'' Wheels	14.00
290	Whitewall Tires, 6.70x15	30.00
313	Powerglide Automatic Transmission	175.00
419	Auxiliary Hardtop	200.00
426	Power Windows	55.00
440	Additional Cove Color	18.00
469A	Optional 245 HP, 283 CI Engine (2x4 Carb)	140.00
469B	Optional 270 HP, 283 CI engine (2x4 Carb)	170.00
579A	Optional 250 HP, 283 CI Engine (Fuel Inj)	450.00
579B	Optional 283 HP, 283 CI Engine (Fuel Inj)	450.00
579E	Optional 283 HP, 283 CI Engine (Fuel Inj)	675.00
473	Power Operated Folding Top Mechanism	130.00
677	Positraction Axle, 3.70:1 Ratio	45.00
678	Positraction Axle, 4.11:1 Ratio	45.00
679	Positraction Axle, 4.56:1 Ratio	45.00
684	Heavy Duty Racing Suspension	725.00
685	4-Speed Transmission	175.00

One of the few ways to differentiate between a 1956 and 1957 model without opening the hood is to compare the inside rearview mirrors. The 1956 at left adjusts with a thumbscrew. The 1957 requires a wrench to loosen a locknut. Author photos.

Fuel-injected models are more responsive and quicker, and are much more expensive. In the past, some owners became disenchanted with the ability of local dealers to service their fuel injection and had the units removed and replaced with carburetors. Rebuilding these fuel-injection systems properly does require expertise and may mean that you'll have to unbolt the unit and ship it to a specialist. But once set up properly, they are reliable and require minimal maintenance.

Both the 1956 and 1957 Corvettes are fine investments. The only negative factor is that prices have already been bid up quite high because enthusiasts sized up these models long ago. Simply put, many believe these to be among history's best all-time sports cars. Without question, the Corvette was grossly underpriced in its day. The logical comparison cars, the Mercedes, Jaguar and Ferrari, were much more expensive. The Corvette was so cheap a lot of people initially discounted it as a serious competitor. It was hard for them to believe the Corvette could have come so far so quickly.

Enthusiasts who want to drive a vintage Corvette daily appreciate the externally opening trunk common to all Corvettes up to the 1962 model. Many also prefer the spare tire location, which is reached by lifting the trunk mat. Post-1962 models have spares located under the car and often requires one to lie on the ground to extract the tire. Author photo.

Unique to the 1956 and 1957 models was an unusual waffle-pattern interior vinyl. Removable hardtops were available for the first time as a factory option in 1956 and the waffle-pattern vinyl was used on the inner top surface as well. Author photos.

The dash of the 1956 and 1957 was similar to the earlier Corvettes and still had all instruments except the speedometer strung out across the center dash area. But the 1956 Corvette had roll-up windows and even offered power-assisted windows as an option. (Note the power window button just forward of the door opening knob.) Author photo.

In the age of massive chrome adornments, the 1956 and 1957 Corvettes somehow managed to emerge with exquisite detailing. Emblems and scripts were understated and items like the exhaust exit and taillight were beautifully executed. Author photos.

1956-1957 Corvette

BASE ENGINE

Type: . . . . .Chevrolet ohv V-8
Bore x stroke, inches: 3.75x3.00 (1956), 3.875x3.00 (1957)
Displacement, inches: 265 (1956), 283 (1957)
Compression ratio: 9.25:1 (1956), 9.5:1 (1957)
Carburetion: . . . . .Single four-barrel carburetor
Horsepower: 210 (1956), 220 (1957)
Distributor: .Single point breaker
Other engines offered:...Higher horsepower variations were available in both 1956 and 1957. See option charts.

CHASSIS AND DRIVETRAIN

Clutch: . . . . .Single dry-plate
Transmission: . . . . .Three-speed manual

Front suspension:...Coil springs, tube-type shock absorbers, stabilizer bar
Rear suspension:...Leaf springs, tube-type shock absorbers, rigid axle
Axle ratio: 3.70:1
Frame: . . . . .Steel box sections, welded

GENERAL:

Wheelbase, inches: 102
Track, front, inches: 57.0
rear, inches: 58.8
Brakes: . . . . .Drum
Tire size, front and rear: 6.70-15
Wheels: . . . . .Steel
Body material: . . . . .Fiberglass
Assembly plant: . . . . .St. Louis, Missouri

Serial Nos. 1958: J58S100001 - J58S109168
          1959: J59S100001 - J59S109670
          1960: 00867S100001 - 00867S110261

There was one problem with building what might have been the world's best production sports car before 1958. How do you make it better?

In 1958 Chevrolet decided to make the Corvette more, well . . . contemporary. Nineteen fifty-eight started what many people now believe was Detroit's worst design era. Great cars, mind you, but dripping with chrome, tailfins and any number of other excesses.

The Corvette managed to avoid tailfins but not much else. The 1956 and 1957 Corvettes were among the cleanest designs ever, but the 1958 turned out just the opposite. It got quad headlights, eighteen fake louvers across the hood, spears down the trunk and lots of chrome. Worst of all, it started a two-decade Corvette weight-gaining trend. The 1958 was the first Corvette to exceed 3,000 pounds.

But there is another side. The 1958 was the tightest, strongest, fastest Corvette yet. Five engines were offered: a standard single four-barrel at 230 horsepower, two dual-carburetor versions at 245 and 270 horsepower, and two fuel-injected versions at 250 and 290 horsepower. The dash was new and grouped all engine-monitoring instruments in front of the driver, a failing of earlier Corvette interiors. General Motors joined the Automobile Manufacturers Association (AMA) ban on racing in 1957, but you'd never know it looking at the 1958 option list.

The 1959 and 1960 models are very similar to each other and both are similar to the 1958, other than being considerably cleaner. Stylists got roasted for the excesses of the 1958 model, so the hood louvers and trunk spears were gone by 1959. Interior vinyl *looked* like interior vinyl in the 1959 and 1960, whereas the 1958 had an unusual pebble grain. Nineteen fifty-nine was the first year for a genuine black interior in a Corvette, though the 1958 had a dark gray unique to the year that can be mistaken for faded black.

The 1959 got a reverse lockout T-shift handle for four-speeds, another Corvette first. The engines were much the same for all years except the top of the line fuel-injected version grew to 315 horsepower in 1960. All three years had seat belts standard; they were dealer-installed in 1956-57 and not generally available before that.

The 1958-60 Corvettes have never really "caught on" and, considering what lies under their criticized exteriors, they're bargains. The 1958 belongs in a

There was no mistaking the 1958 Corvette. Chevrolet photo.

Although the 1958 Corvette outsold any previous year, the model was criticized because of design excesses and for starting a weight-gaining Corvette trend. Nonetheless, there are some who predict the 1958 will become a great collector car because of the controversy that has always surrounded it. It remains to be seen. Author photos.

category by itself, definitely a love-it or hate-it car. In the view of some, the controversy surrounding the car since its introduction just adds to its charm. For others, the cleaner 1959 and 1960 models, the last "classic" Corvettes with consistent round fender shapes front and rear, are the most desirable.

High-performance Corvettes always score well with collectors looking at the investment angle, but this isn't a critical consideration for this series of Corvettes. The Corvette's option list, as well as color and trim choices, was getting better than ever. By 1960 there were some terrific combinations and it became clear that Chevrolet was going to let customers tailor the Corvette to their own liking, in true American auto industry tradition. Turquoise convertible top? You could get it in 1959.

The Powerglide automatic transmission and power windows were available in these models, but power steering, power brakes and air conditioning were not. Like the Corvettes before them, the 1958-1960 Corvettes tend to feel harsh and heavy compared to contemporary sports cars, particularly if fitted with original style tires.

Corvette production was growing but still modest by most standards. In 1958, 9,168 were made. It increased to 9,670 in 1959 and to 10,261 in 1960. For someone who likes Corvettes of this period, there are no real disadvantages of ownership of any of these models other than an appreciation rate that historically has not kept pace with the rest of the Corvette fleet. For the gambler, the 1958 is the closest thing to a "sleeper" of all classic Corvette years.

In its advertising, Chevrolet pointed out that the "new assist bar aids passenger." Chevrolet photo.

1958 Corvette Colors/Options

Color Code	Body Color	Soft Top Color
None	Charcoal	Black/White
None	Snowcrest White	Black/White/Beige
None	Silver Blue	White/Beige
None	Regal Turquoise	Black/White
None	Panama Yellow	Black/White
None	Signet Red	Black/White

INTERIOR COLORS: Charcoal, Blue-Green, Red

Order #	Item Description	Sticker Price
867	Base Corvette Convertible	3591.00
101	Heater	96.85
102	Signal Seeking AM Radio	144.45
107	Parking Brake Alarm	5.40
108	Courtesy Lights	6.50
109	Windshield Washer	16.15
276	5 15x5.5'' Wheels	NC
290	Whitewall Tires, 6.70x15	31.55
313	Powerglide Automatic Transmission	188.30
419	Auxiliary Hardtop	215.20
426	Electric Power Windows	59.20
440	Additional Cove Color	16.15
469	Optional 245 HP, 283 CI Engine (2x4 Carb)	150.65
469C	Optional 270 HP, 283 CI Engine (2x4 Carb)	182.95
579	Optional 250 HP, 283 CI Engine (Fuel Inj)	484.20
579D	Optional 290 HP, 283 CI Engine (Fuel Inj)	484.20
473	Power Operated Folding Top Mechanism	139.90
677	Positraction Axle, 3.70:1 Ratio	48.45
678	Positraction Axle, 4.11:1 Ratio	48.45
679	Positraction Axle, 4.56:1 Ratio	48.45
684	Heavy Duty Brakes and Suspension	780.10
685	4-Speed Transmission	215.20

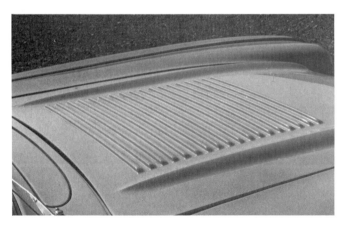

The dual headlights and massive bumpers got their share of criticism, but it was the "washboard" hood and chrome trunk spears that seemed to rankle enthusiasts most. These features were unique to the 1958 Corvette as both were dropped the following year. Author photos.

Corvette designers heard the criticism of earlier Corvette instrument layouts and redesigned the 1958 dash with all instruments except the clock right in front of the driver. Author photo.

The 1958 inner door panel was a complicated affair, but did include reflector buttons, a Corvette first. Note also the pebble grain, unique to the 1958 model. Author photo.

1959 Corvette Colors/Options

Color Code	Body Color	Soft Top Color
None	Tuxedo Black	Black/White
None	Classic Cream	Black/White
None	Frost Blue	White/Blue
None	Crown Sapphire	White/Turquoise
None	Roman Red	Black/White
None	Snowcrest White	Black/White/Tan/Blue
None	Inca Silver	Black/White

INTERIOR COLORS: Black, Blue, Red, Turquoise

Order #	Item Description	Sticker Price
867	Base Corvette Convertible	3875.00
—	Additional Cove Color	16.15
101	Heater	102.25
102	Signal Seeking AM Radio	149.80
107	Parking Brake Alarm	5.40
108	Courtesy Light	6.50
109	Windshield Washers	16.15
261	Sunshades	10.80
276	5 15x5.5'' Wheels	nc
290	Whitewall Tires, 6.70x15	31.55
313	Powerglide Automatic Transmission	199.10
419	Auxiliary Hardtop	236.75
426	Electric Power Windows	59.20
269	Optional 245 HP, 283 CI Engine (2x4 Carb)	150.65
469C	Optional 270 HP, 283 CI Engine (2x4 Carb)	182.95
579	Optional 250 HP, 283 CI Engine (Fuel Inj)	484.20
579D	Optional 290 HP, 283 CI Engine (Fuel Inj)	484.20
473	Power Operated Folding Top Mechanism	139.90
675	Positraction Axle, Optional Ratio	48.45
684	Heavy Duty Brakes and Suspension	425.05
685	4-Speed Transmission	188.30
686	Metallic Brakes	26.90

1960 Corvette Colors/Options

Color Code	Body Color	Soft Top Color
None	Tuxedo Black	Black/White/Blue
None	Tasco Turquoise	Black/White/Blue
None	Horizon Blue	Black/White/Blue
None	Honduras Maroon	Black
None	Roman Red	Black/White
None	Ermine White	Black/White/Blue
None	Sateen Silver	Black/White/Blue
None	Cascade Green	Black/White/Blue

INTERIOR COLORS: Black, Blue, Red, Turquoise

Order #	Item Description	Sticker Price
867	Base Corvette Convertible	3872.00
—	Additional Cove Color	16.15
101	Heater	102.25
102	Signal Seeking AM Radio	137.75
107	Parking Brake Alarm	5.40
108	Courtesy Light	6.50
109	Windshield Washers	16.15
121	Temperature Controlled Radiator Fan	21.55
261	Sunshades	10.80
276	5 15x5.5'' Wheels	nc
290	Whitewall Tires, 6.70x15.4-ply	31.55
313	Powerglide Automatic Transmission	199.10
419	Auxiliary Hardtop	236.75
426	Electric Power Windows	59.20
469	Optional 245 HP, 283 CI Engine (2x4 Carb)	150.65
469C	Optional 270 HP, 283 CI Engine (2x4 Carb)	182.95
579	Optional 275 HP, 283 CI Engine (Fuel Inj)	484.20
579D	Optional 315 HP, 283 CI Engine (Fuel Inj)	484.20
473	Power Operated Folding Top Mechanism	139.90
675	Positraction Axle, Optional Ratio	43.05
685	4-Speed Transmission	188.30
686	Metallic Brakes	26.90
687	Heavy Duty Brakes and Suspension	333.60
1408	5 6.70x15 Nylon Tires	15.75
1625A	24 Gallon Fuel Tank	161.40

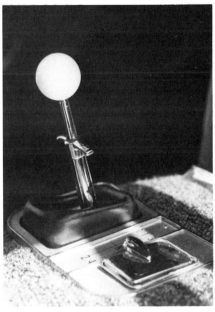

The 1958 four-speed shifter at left was the same as the 1957, but in 1959 (right) the reverse lock-out "T" bar was incorporated. The chrome shift knob shown in the 1958 is owner-added. Original equipment was a white plastic knob. Author photos.

The 1959 and 1960 models were virtually indistinguishable and both bear strong resemblance to the 1958 model. These Corvettes were excellent performers but their styling has kept prices reasonable. Some are excellent values today. Chevrolet photo.

Both 1959 and 1960 Corvettes had clean hoods and trunks, surely a response to criticism of the 1958 models. Note the slotted hubcap design, which was common to all Corvettes in the 1958 through 1960 period except for early 1958's which did not have the slots. Author photos.

Corvettes and women always seemed to go together nicely, a fact not lost upon those responsible for Chevrolet advertising. 1960 shown. Chevrolet photo.

1958-1959-1960 Corvette

BASE ENGINE

Type: . . . . Chevrolet ohv V-8
Bore x stroke, inches: . . . . .3.875 x 3.00
Displacement, inches: 283
Compression ratio:. 9.5:1
Carburetion:. . . . . Single four-barrel carburetor
Horsepower:. 230
Distributor: . . . . Single point breaker
Other engines offered:...Higher horsepower variations were available in 1958, 1959 and 1960. See option charts.

CHASSIS AND DRIVETRAIN

Clutch:. . . . . .Single dry-plate
Transmission:. . . . . .Three-speed manual

Front suspension:...Coil springs, tube-type shock absorbers, stabilizer bar
Rear suspension:...Leaf springs, tube-type shock absorbers, rigid axle
Axle ratio: 3.70:1
Frame: . . . . Steel box sections, welded

GENERAL:

Wheelbase, inches: 102
Track, front, inches:. 57.0
   rear, inches: 58.8
Brakes: . . . . .Drum
Tire size, front and rear: 6.70-15
Wheels: . . . . .Steel
Body material: . . . . .Fiberglass
Assembly plant: . . . . .St. Louis, Missouri

CHAPTER 5
1961-1962 CORVETTE

 (Fuel Injection)

Serial Nos. 1961: 10867S100001 - 10867S110939
1962: 20867S100001 - 20867S114531

"Classic" is a term used by Corvette enthusiasts to denote Corvettes built up to and including the 1962 model. All of these share two main characteristics cherished by classic loyalists: All have external trunks and all have solid rear axles (as compared to the independent rear suspensions common to all 1963 and later Corvettes).

The trunk aspect permits things like golf clubs and other necessities to be loaded from the rear of the car and locked out of sight. This is a feature Corvettes were never to see again, unless the definition of trunk is stretched to include the opening rear window started by the 1982 Collector Edition.

The solid rear axle is not state-of-the-art design but, characteristic of the period, it is very durable and it imparts a "feel" to classic Corvettes which later models just don't have. Some like the feel, some don't. Those who do, think the feel plus the high "elbow out the window" seating of the classics add up to an unbeatable sports car driving environment.

For those who love classic Corvettes, the 1961 and 1962 models have a lot going for them. They're the last of the breed and definitely the best in some ways. The overall quality of construction of the 1961-62 Corvettes was as good as any in Corvette history, especially if you limit consideration to those built in St. Louis. Production jumped dramatically in following years and took its inevitable toll in quality.

As performers, the cars were fierce, the best yet in the Corvette's evolution. A little history lesson is required to understand why.

General Motors joined other manufacturers in banning factory participation in auto racing in 1957. Zora Arkus-Duntov, unofficially the Corvette's chief engineer by then, was always a believer in building two versions of a sports car—one to go racing and another to sell to the public. With his racing wings clipped, Duntov had to try building one Corvette that could satisfy both camps. The result was a production Corvette for racers that was a little less than they needed, but a production Corvette for consumers that was more than they ever expected.

This effect started showing up in the 1959 model but really began to be strongly felt in the 1961. All 1961 Corvettes got aluminum radiators, previously standard only with hot "Duntov" cam engines. The 1961 also got a temperature-controlled fan behind the radiator that didn't drain power unless necessary. The four-speed transmission case was changed to aluminum in 1961 and even the Powerglide case got the aluminum treatment for 1962.

1961 Corvette. Chevrolet photos.

The 1961 Corvette was the last available with a contrasting color in the side cove area. Stylists toned down the front end by painting the headlight bezels body color (previously chrome) and replacing the grille teeth with fine mesh. The rear was all-new, borrowed from the Sting Ray design still two years away. Chevrolet photos.

1961 Corvette Colors/Options

Color Code	Body Color	Soft Top Color
None	Tuxedo Black	Black/White
None	Ermine White	Black/White
None	Roman Red	Black/White
None	Sateen Silver	Black/White
None	Jewel Blue	Black/White
None	Fawn Beige	Black/White
None	Honduras Maroon	Black/White

INTERIOR COLORS: Black, Red, Fawn, Blue

Order #	Item Description	Sticker Price
867	Base Corvette Convertible	3934.00
—	Additional Cove Color	16.15
101	Heater	102.25
102	Signal Seeking AM Radio	137.75
276	5 15x5.5'' Wheels	nc
290	Whitewall Tires, 6.70x15	31.55
313	Powerglide Automatic Transmission	199.10
419	Auxiliary Hardtop	236.75
426	Electric Power Windows	59.20
441	Direct Flow Exhaust System	nc
469	Optional 245 HP, 283 CI Engine (2x4 Carb)	150.65
468	Optional 270 HP, 283 CI Engine (2x4 Carb)	182.95
353	Optional 275 HP, 283 CI Engine (Fuel Inj)	484.20
354	Optional 315 HP, 283 CI Engine (Fuel Inj)	484.20
473	Power Operated Folding Top Mechanism	161.40
675	Positraction Axle, Optional Ratio	43.05
685	4-Speed Transmission	188.30
686	Metallic Brakes	37.70
687	Heavy Duty Brakes and Suspension	333.60
1408	5 6.70x15 Nylon Tires	15.75
1625	24 Gallon Fuel Tank	161.40

The 1961 and 1962 Corvettes continued with features started by the 1956 model, including a lockable storage area between the seats and optional power windows. The restored 1962 Corvette pictured has genuine stitching in its seats and door panels, but the originals had simulated stitches. Author photos.

The chassis of the 1961-62 was the same as in previous years, but the fiberglass body was reworked. Quad headlights remained, but the big grille teeth were replaced by a tasteful mesh. The 1961 still had the side cove outlined by a bright molding (started in 1956) and the area inside the cove could be ordered in a color contrasting the body color. But in 1962 the bright molding was replaced with a highlight lip. Two-tones were gone from the Corvette scene until the silver anniversary paint scheme arrived in 1978.

The rear end styling of the 1961-62 was changed extensively and drew mixed reviews. The design was obviously grafted from the new Sting Ray scheduled for 1963 introduction. It incorporated a four-taillight set up; now a Corvette trademark, but a first for the Corvette in 1961.

Viewed on its own, the rear end styling is very nice. The controversy centered on the mismatched look, front to rear. The front was a carryover of the old Corvette rounded look, but the rear was a preview of the crisper "beltline" styling of the Sting Rays to come. Two concepts or not, stylists pulled it off quite well and these Corvettes look fine today. And the restyled rear added twenty percent to the trunk volume.

All engines in 1961 continued to be based on Chevy's 283-cubic-inch V-8. But in 1962, displacement went up to 327 cubic inches. In fact, even though the 1963 Corvette made its debut as an all-new model, the engines were exact carryovers from 1962. As was the case with all Corvettes built up to and including the 1962 model, power steering, power brakes and air conditioning were not available.

Both the 1961 and 1962 Corvettes are excellent investments. Each does have its advantages. They both can lay claim to being the hottest performer in the classic era, a slight edge going to the 1962 with its larger-displacement engines. With its wide whitewalls and two-tone paint treatment, the 1961 is more reminiscent of earlier Corvettes. The whitewalls were thinner in 1962 and this, plus the single body color, makes it more the harbinger of things to come while still maintaining all the attributes classic Corvette lovers love. It's a draw.

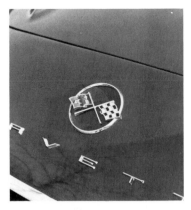

There were subtle emblem changes between 1961 and 1962. The nose emblem of the 1961 was a crossed flag over a "V," but the 1962 was a crossed flag inside a circle. The rear emblems were similar except that the 1961 had a spun silver background and the 1962 background was black. Author photos.

1962 Corvette Colors/Options

Color Code	Body Color	Soft Top Color
None	Tuxedo Black	Black/White
None	Fawn Beige	Black/White
None	Roman Red	Black/White
None	Ermine White	Black/White
None	Almond Beige	Black/White
None	Sateen Silver	Black/White
None	Honduras Maroon	Black/White

INTERIOR COLORS: Black, Red, Fawn

Order #	Item Description	Sticker Price
867	Base Corvette Convertible	4038.00
102	Signal Seeking AM Radio	137.75
276	5 15x5.5'' Wheels	nc
313	Powerglide Automatic Transmission	199.10
419	Auxiliary Hardtop	236.75
426	Electric Power Windows	59.20
441	Direct Flow Exhaust System	nc
473	Power Operated Folding Top Mechanism	139.90
488	24 Gallon Fuel Tank	118.40
583	Optional 300 HP, 327 CI Engine	53.80
396	Optional 340 HP, 327 CI Engine	107.60
582	Optional 370 HP, 327 CI Engine (Fuel Inj)	484.20
675	Positraction Rear Axle	43.05
685	4-Speed Transmission	188.30
686	Metallic Brakes	37.70
687	Heavy Duty Brakes and Suspension	333.60
1832	Whitewall Tires, 6.70x15	31.55
1833	Nylon Tires, 6.70x15	15.70

Though very similar to 1961, the 1962 Corvette had its differences. It was the first year for thin whitewall tires (between ⅞" and 1"), and the first with the higher displacement, 327-cubic-inch engines. The bright molding was removed from the side cove area and the cove could no longer be ordered in a contrasting color. Author photos.

A lot ended in 1962. This was the last Corvette with an externally opening trunk (excluding the rear window hatches of the new generation.)
And it was the last Corvette with exposed headlights. Chevrolet and
author photos.

This staged promotional photo illustrates the high seating characteristics of all Corvettes built before 1963. This, plus a wide upper door section, created a comfortable "arm out the window" driving style unmatched by any Corvette built since. Chevrolet photo.

The 1961 and 1962 (1962 shown) instrument cluster changed little from that introduced in 1958. Author photo.

1961-1962 Corvette

BASE ENGINE
Type: . . . . Chevrolet ohv V-8
Bore x stroke , inches: 3.875 x 3.0 (1961), 4.0 x 3.25 (1962)
Displacement, inches: 283 (1961), 327 (1962)
Compression ratio: 9.5:1 (1961), 10.5:1 (1962)
Carburetion: . . . . .Single four-barrel carburetor
Horsepower: 230 (1961), 250 (1962)
Distributor: . . . . .Single point breaker
Other engines offered: . . .Higher horsepower variations were
    available in both 1961 and 1962. See option charts.

CHASSIS AND DRIVETRAIN
Clutch: . . . . .Single dry-plate
Transmission: .Three-speed manual

Front suspension: . . .Coil springs, tube-type shock absorbers,
    stabilizer bar
Rear suspension: . . .Leaf springs, tube-type shock absorbers,
    rigid axle
Axle ratio: 3.36:1
Frame: . . . . .Steel box sections, welded
GENERAL:
Wheelbase, inches: 102
Track, front, inches: 57.0
    rear, inches: 58.8
Brakes: . . . . .Drum
Tire size, front and rear: 6.70-15
Wheels: . . . . .Steel
Body material: . . . . .Fiberglass
Assembly plant: . . . . .St. Louis, Missouri

CHAPTER 6
1963-1964 CORVETTE

⭐⭐⭐⭐ (Fuel Injection)
⭐⭐⭐⭐⭐ (1963 Coupe)

Serial Nos. 1963: 30867S100001 - 30867S121513*
1964: 40867S100001 - 40867S122229*
(*for coupes, fourth digit is a 3)

Chevrolet uncorked a dandy in 1963. The engines and transmissions carried over from 1962, but otherwise the Corvette was brand new. It had a beautiful new body, available for the first time as either a closed coupe or open convertible. The chassis was new and included independent rear suspension and a novel, single transverse rear spring. What a car.

And what an introduction! Cloaked in secrecy right up to release, the Corvette exploded onto the market. There wasn't much dickering for a few dollars off sticker prices. These were instant hits and in tremendous demand from the first day.

This was one of those rare times when everything came together just right. The Corvette engine was already highly thought of. After all, the Chevy V-8 is one of the all-time favorites and the Corvette had the Chevy engine in its best form. A wrecked Corvette was worth its weight in gold for the engine alone.

Prior to 1963, Corvettes were criticized for having an outdated chassis and inconsistent styling that, the 1956-57 models excluded, were hard to rave about. Styling is a subjective thing, but the chassis complaints were certainly valid. The first Corvettes were designed around a chassis which some people felt was already obsolete.

All this ceased in 1963. The chassis which made its debut in 1963 was good enough to last almost untouched right through the 1982 model. And the body styling was on a par with anything anywhere. This new body/chassis combination left critics with very little to criticize. The 1963 could have done with a few less styling frills, and drum brakes were still being used to stop very potent machines. That was about it, and Chevrolet took care of these shortcomings in short order.

The styling of the 1963 Corvette was a shock, but not a total surprise to real auto buffs. The Corvette look was influenced strongly by a one-off race car called the Mitchell Sting Ray. The story of how this racer came about and the part it played in the development of the beautiful production Corvettes starting with the 1963, is a great part of Corvette folklore.

The story centers on two events and three men. The events were the Automobile Manufacturers Association ban on racing in 1957, with which General Motors went along, and the promotion of William L. Mitchell as successor to Harley Earl as head of all GM styling. The men were Mitchell, his chief Corvette stylist Larry Shinoda, and Zora Arkus-Duntov.

Duntov was the most pro-racing individual of some influence in the modern history of General Motors. He had personally raced in Europe with and against

1963 Corvette "Split Window" Coupe. Chevrolet photo.

The Corvettes starting with the 1963 model had a history before they were even introduced, thanks to the Mitchell racing Sting Ray. This gorgeous vehicle was campaigned on the race circuit under the sponsorship of Bill Mitchell, GM's vice president in charge of design, four years before the production vehicles based on it were released. Chevrolet photo.

In 1963, Zora Arkus-Duntov decided to end the racetrack domination of the Ford-powered Cobra by building 125 lightweight (1908 lbs.) "Grand Sport" Corvettes. Chevrolet management approved but GM corporate did not and Duntov's program was stopped after only five cars were built. Three were immediately sold to private individuals and made their way to racetracks with some success despite not being equipped with the 550 horsepower, cast-aluminum hemi V-8 Duntov had planned. Duntov held back two cars in reserve in case the corporate winds shifted again. He changed these from coupes to convertibles but wasn't allowed to go racing, so these were also sold. All five Grand Sports survive today in private hands and occasionally one is for sale. It's difficult to figure out what one is worth, though asking prices have ranged as high as $1-million. That's a little out of reach for most of us, but we can all dream. And a Grand Sport tops the most wanted list of many Corvette enthusiasts. Chevrolet photos.

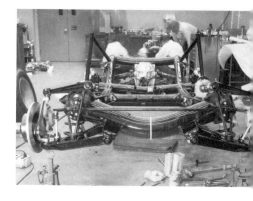

the best cars in the world and he was convinced the Corvette could and should dominate racing worldwide.

In order to accomplish this lofty task, Duntov figured a special Corvette racer would be needed for events like Sebring and Le Mans so he built something called the Corvette SS for the 1957 season.

The SS was approved by GM management, but Duntov's budget called for just one SS to be built. The brass wanted the SS to look nice for fan appeal, and Duntov realized that it could get hung up in Styling. So he secretly built an extra SS chassis and dumped an ugly fiberglass shell over it in order to have something for shakedown tests. The appearance of the shakedown car earned it the nickname "mule."

Duntov was right about the real SS getting bogged down in Styling. The SS arrived for its debut at Sebring in 1957 at the very last minute with stylists still working on it in the transport van. To the surprise of no one, it failed early in the race. The SS and the mule (which tested very well at Sebring and was actually faster) were shipped back to Detroit where Duntov planned to rework both of them for entry later in the year at Le Mans. But then the AMA ban came along and ended the SS forever.

But not the mule.

We now switch to the Mitchell-Shinoda side of the story. William L. Mitchell replaced Harley Earl as head of all GM styling in 1958. Earl was responsible for starting the Corvette in the first place and Mitchell loved it equally. Mitchell thought it essential for the Corvette to have a racing heritage, AMA ban or no AMA ban. He also wanted Chevrolet's image leader to bear his styling influence. He hatched an ingenious plan.

Mitchell knew that the mule was wasting away in a warehouse and that it was a wolf in sheep's clothing, a potential champion. Mitchell persuaded Ed Cole, Chevrolet's general manager and a race-lover himself, to allow a secret Chevrolet styling studio to rebody the mule and turn it loose on the track. To get around the AMA ban, Mitchell paid General Motors one dollar for the car and campaigned it as the Mitchell Sting Ray, with Dick Thompson driving. There was considerable personal time given by Mitchell and his "crew" but this was very definitely a corporate project. Everyone involved just snickers about it today.

Mitchell turned to his secret studio, managed by Larry Shinoda, to create the body for the Sting Ray and Shinoda and company created a masterpiece. Simply put, the original Sting Ray racer is one of the neatest cars ever. The reaction of everyone who saw it was just what Mitchell had hoped for and he turned Shinoda's studio loose on adapting the design to a new Corvette production model for 1963. The Sting Ray name appropriately captured the aggressive look of the racer's flowing fender lines and was used for the production cars.

Nineteen sixty-three was the year of the split-window coupe. From the first moment Mitchell saw the split rear window proposal in Shinoda's studio, he liked it and adamantly insisted it stay in. Others, including Duntov, said it was dumb and blocked rear vision severely. Duntov and those who agreed with him got their way in 1964 when the split was removed. Before he passed away, Mitchell admitted the split wasn't very practical; he just liked the way it looked.

One thing is for sure. The 1963 coupe is now one of the greatest collector Corvettes of all. It's hard to believe that in the sixties people actually chopped the split out of 1963 coupes and put in glass from later models. A few years later they were reinstalling the split glass. And more than one 1964 Corvette has acquired the split and changed its identity.

Everything about the 1963 Corvette was new, including interior vinyl trim. A leather interior option became available for the first time in a Corvette in 1963, but it included only the seats, and just the tan color could be ordered in leather. In 1964, all interior color choices could be ordered in either vinyl or extra-cost leather. Author photo.

The Corvette fuel-injected engine continued to be available in both 1963 and 1964. The system was similar to previous years, but a new-style air cleaner and doghouse (plenum chamber) made their debut in 1963. The 1963 engines carried over from 1962, and all were 327 cid. The same was true of 1964 except that horsepower ratings of two engines were increased. Author photo.

The 1963 and 1964 Corvettes are very similar, but the 1963 started the show and it commands higher prices. The difference between convertibles is sometimes negligible, but there's no comparison between coupes. The 1964 is every bit as good a car, but that twenty-inch split down the 1963's rear glass makes it worth more, sometimes fifty percent more. It's nuts but it's true. And it probably won't change.

The 1963 Corvette started the hidden headlight trend for Corvettes. In the 1963, the revolving unit was fiberglass on all but very late production cars. The late ones and all later Sting Rays had metal shells.

Real "knock off" wheels made the option list in 1963, but it's doubtful that any were actually factory-installed until 1964 due to leak problems. The wheels have become so popular that reproductions of the wheels are now available. The repros cost less than $1,000 per set. Originals are more desirable and cost five to ten times as much, depending on condition. The real knock-off style was used through the 1966 model, but only the 1963-64 wheel style was left unpainted between the fins.

Air conditioning became a Corvette option for the first time in 1963 but late introduction resulted in less than two-percent usage in 1963 models. A few more have been "built" by owners. Nineteen sixty-three also marked the first availability of power steering and power brakes in Corvettes.

Leather seat material was also introduced in 1963. It was only available in tan, but in 1964 all interior colors could be ordered in leather. Trim code tags under the gloveboxes of 1963 and newer Corvettes specify not only the interior color but material as well. Changing worn-out vinyl seats to leather doesn't lower a Corvette's value greatly because it's easy to change back to vinyl, but a Corvette with leather seats which is properly coded for leather is definitely more valuable.

Horsepower ratings for two engines increased in 1964. The solid lifter, non-injected engine increased from 340 to 365 horsepower. The fuel-injected engine went from 360 to 375 horsepower.

The 1963 had two hood depressions with fake vent plates in each. These plates were styled to look like the functional hood vents of the Mitchell Sting Ray racer. In 1964, the plates were eliminated, but the hood depressions remained. Both years had a thirty-six-gallon fuel tank available as an option in coupes. The tanks ate up most of the storage space behind the seats, but Corvettes with them are prized by collectors. Both 1963 and 1964 models had AM-FM radios as options, except for early 1963's, which were signal-seeking AM types.

Production for the two years was almost equal. The 21,513 made in 1963 were slightly surpassed by 1964's 22,229. The coupe-to-convertible mix in 1963 was nearly even, but 1964 coupe production was only thirty-seven percent.

Some 1963 and 1964 models are excellent investments; but be selective. The 1963 coupe is one of the fastest appreciating Corvettes. Combined with desirable options like fuel-injection or air conditioning, the split-window coupe makes a prized collector car.

In any measurable way, the 1964 is as good a car as the 1963, but it doesn't share the same mystique nor the same appreciation rate. Granted, some specially equipped 1964's are very valuable; but when comparing similar cars the 1963 will sell for more. The 1964 is caught in an unfortunate squeeze. It followed the lead car in what many consider to be the best Corvette series, but it preceded the model year that brought four-wheel disc brakes to the Corvette.

The price differential between 1963 and 1964 models is substantial, but less so when comparing convertibles. In investment terms, it would be most accurate to lump the 1963 convertibles in with both 1964 body styles, then consider the split-window coupe in a category by itself.

Is the 1963 coupe really worth the extra expense? Not from any objective standpoint. But it has a unique place in Corvette history and nothing else will ever quite equal it. It's worth it.

1963-1964 Corvette

BASE ENGINE

Type: . . . . .Chevrolet ohv V-8
Bore x stroke, inches: . . . . .4.00 x 3.25
Displacement, inches: 327
Compression ratio: 10.5:1
Carburetion: . . . . .Single four-barrel carburetor
Horsepower: 250
Distributor: . . . . .Single point breaker
Other engines offered:. . .Higher horsepower variations were available in both 1963 and 1964. See option charts.

CHASSIS AND DRIVETRAIN

Clutch: . . . . .Single dry-plate
Transmission: . . . . .Three-speed manual

Front suspension:. . .Coil springs, tube-type shock absorbers, stabilizer bar
Rear suspension:. . .Single transverse leaf spring, tube-type shock absorbers, independent with lateral struts
Axle ratio: 3.36:1
Frame: .Steel box sections, welded
GENERAL:
Wheelbase, inches: 98
Track, front, inches: 56.25
rear, inches: 57.0
Brakes: . . . . .Drum
Tire size, front and rear: . . . . .6.70 x 15
Wheels: . . . . .Steel
Body material: . . . . .Fiberglass
Assembly plant: . . . . .St. Louis, Missouri

The 1963 Corvette wasn't the first in automotive history to feature hidden headlights, but it certainly started the modern trend to use them. The 1963-67 units were each operated by electric motors. The units were the same for 1963-67 except that the headlight housings were fiberglass in the 1963 (except for a few late cars) and metal in all others. Author photos.

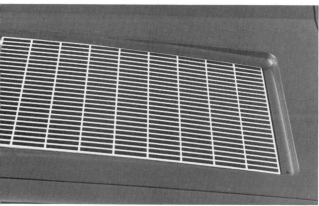

The 1963 Corvette instrument cluster was a little fancy, but drew raves for its functional layout. The silver center cones and silver outer bezels changed to black for the 1964 model. The hood grilles were styled to look like the functional heat exhausts of the racing Sting Ray. The side fender ducts were also nonfunctional in both 1963 and 1964 models. Author photos.

All 1963 through 1967 Corvettes had beautiful removable hardtops available for the convertible models (1964 shown). The 1964 had hood depressions but no fake vent trim like the 1963. Author photos.

1964 Corvette Colors/Options

Color Code	Body Color	Soft Top Color
900	Tuxedo Black	Black/White/Beige
936	Ermine White	Black/White/Beige
923	Riverside Red	Black/White/Beige
940	Satin Silver	Black/White/Beige
912	Silver Blue	Black/White/Beige
916	Daytona Blue	Black/White/Beige
932	Saddle Tan	Black/White/Beige

INTERIOR COLORS: Black, Red, Silver, White, Saddle, Dark Blue

Order #	Item Description	Sticker Price
837	Base Corvette Sport Coupe	4252.00
867	Base Corvette Convertible	4037.00
—	Genuine Leather Seat Trim	80.70
A01	Soft Ray Tinted Glass, All Windows	16.15
A02	Soft Ray Tinted Glass, Windshield	10.80
A31	Electric Power Windows	59.20
C07	Auxiliary Hardtop (for roadster)	236.75
C48	Heater and Defroster Deletion (credit)	−100.00
C60	Air Conditioning (not available with L84)	421.80
F40	Special Front and Rear Suspension	37.70
G81	Positraction Rear Axle, All Ratios	43.05
G91	Special Highway 3.08:1 Axle	2.20
J50	Power Brakes	43.05
J56	Special Sintered Metallic Brake Package	629.50
J65	Sintered Metallic Brakes (power)	53.80
K66	Transistor Ignition System	65.35
L75	Optional 300 HP, 327 CI Engine	53.80
L76	Optional 365 HP, 327 CI Engine	107.60
L84	Optional 375 HP, 327 CI Engine (Fuel Inj)	538.00
M20	4-Speed Transmission	188.30
M35	Powerglide Automatic	199.10
N03	36 Gallon Fuel Tank (coupe only)	202.30
N11	Off Road Exhaust System	37.70
N40	Power Steering	75.35
P48	Special Cast Aluminum Knock-Off Wheels	322.80
P91	Blackwall Nylon Tires, 6.70x15	15.70
P92	Whitewall Rayon Tires, 6.70x15	31.85
T86	Back Up Lamps	10.80
U69	AM-FM Radio	176.50

Cast aluminum wheels with real knock-off hubs were offered for 1963-64 Corvettes, though it's likely none were factory-installed on any 1963 models due to leak problems. The surface between the fins was unpainted on the 1963-64 style. The wheels' popularity has resulted in their remanufacture, but originals had thinner fins and other subtle differences and are far more valuable than the repros. Author photo.

 (Fuel Injection, Big Block)

Serial Nos. 1965: 194675S100001 - 194675S123562*
1966: 194676S100001 - 194676S127720*
(*for coupes, fourth digit is a 3)

Chevrolet did the impossible in 1965. It made the Corvette better again.

The big news for the 1965 Corvette was a four-wheel disc brake system. Previous Corvettes had used a drum brake setup front and rear that was lifted from the Chevy passenger car line. That was fine for the first Blue Flame models, but Corvettes were getting faster every year and the brakes just stayed the same. Ten years into production, the 150-horsepower Blue Flame had given way to a 1963 model that could be purchased right out of the show room with 340 horsepower. A sintered metallic brake option had been offered but these were racing brakes that had to be "heated up" to work properly. They were not practical for street use.

Chevy engineers didn't fool around with an interim disc front/drum rear arrangement. They went right to discs at all four wheels. In so doing, they catapulted the Corvette right into the ranks of the world's best cars in fadeproof stopping power. The system remained virtually unchanged in every Corvette built through the end of 1982, and the 1982 model still stopped with the best.

The new disc brake system was standard equipment starting with the 1965 Corvette, but for a while Chevrolet offered a "delete cost" option of drum brakes to reduce inventory. For a measly savings of $64.50, it's difficult to understand the logic of specifying the drums, unless for their simplicity and anticipated lower maintenance costs.

As it turned out, the discs did develop reliability problems. The system was complex, using four pistons driving dual calipers at each wheel. As pads wore, piston seals encountered areas of their steel bores which were subject to corrosion. With sixteen pistons per car, leaks were all but inevitable. In one of the great mysteries of all time, Chevrolet did nothing about the problem until it completely redesigned the brakes with aluminum calipers for its all-new 1984 model.

The leak-prone calipers for 1965 Corvettes turned into a gigantic headache for Corvette owners. The corroded steel caliper bores could be honed, but it was a temporary fix. New calipers from GM were expensive and prone to the same problems after they were in service. In retrospect, that 1965 drum brake substitution option didn't look so dumb after all.

Had Corvettes of the era not developed such a cult following, the brake problem would never have been solved. But the cult did develop and if GM wouldn't solve it, enthusiasts would. And they did.

The 1965 Corvette was the last one available with the fuel-injection system developed by Zora Arkus-Duntov and John Dolza. It has been said many times that fuel injection was replaced during the 1965 model year by the 396 cid "big-block" motors, but records now show that fuel injection was available until near the end of the model run. Author photo.

The 1965 Corvette was the last with fuel injection available and the first with disc brakes. The combination of these two make a terrific and widely acknowledged collector car. Author photo.

The fix turned out to be stainless steel inserts for the caliper bores. There are several aftermarket companies doing this now, some good and some not, but the good ones produce a product that is a lifetime cure and is so guaranteed.

If a disc brake Corvette you're considering for purchase has leaky calipers or originals that haven't started leaking yet, plan to spend about $600 for a permanent fix. That will include sleeving your calipers, new pads and a switch to silicone fluid.

Sadly, fuel-injection was phased out by the end of 1965 production. Its high cost had prevented the degree of market penetration Chevrolet deemed necessary to justify its production. Its replacement, though both were available simultaneously for a time, was the 396-cubic-inch "big-block" with 425 horsepower. Brutal.

The 1965 Corvette enjoys several distinctions. It is the first with disc brakes and big-block motors. It's the last with fuel-injection available, creating just one year that both fuel-injection and disc brakes could be had on the same Corvette. This is a very desirable combination, one that Zora Arkus-Duntov once told an interviewer was the Corvette's zenith from an engineering standpoint.

The 1965 body was a carryover from the previous year, but there were differences. The indentations were removed from the 1965 hood, but models with 396-cubic-inch engines (427 in 1966) received special hoods with newly designed air scoops. The horizontal side fender indentions of the 1963-64 models were replaced by vertical functional slots in 1965 and 1966 models.

Instruments in 1963 and 1964 had long, bent needles; but in 1965 they were changed to a flat dial/straight needle design with strong aircraft design influence. Seats were redesigned in 1965 for better support and the interior door panels starting in 1965 became one-piece molded units, replacing the vinyl-on-fiberboard type of earlier years.

The 1966 was a near twin to the 1965. There were trim changes, an extra batch of pleats in the seats to cure splitting problems and a plated cast grille to replace the earlier extruded aluminum units.

Beautiful side-mounted exhaust systems could be ordered on both years as could telescopic steering columns. A Corvette first and last, a genuine teak steering wheel was optional on both years but on no others. Another Corvette first for both years was the availability of gold-stripe tires. Blackwall tires were still standard and whitewalls were available, too.

1965-1966 Corvette

BASE ENGINE

Type: . . . . Chevrolet ohv V-8
Bore x stroke, inches: 4.00x3.25
Displacement, inches: 327
Compression ratio: 10.5:1 (1965), 10.25:1 (1966)
Carburetion: . . . . Single four-barrel carburetor
Horsepower: 250
Distributor: . . . . Single point breaker
Other engines offered: . . . Higher horsepower variations were available in both 1965 and 1966. See option charts.

CHASSIS AND DRIVETRAIN

Clutch: . . . . Single dry-plate
Transmission: . . . . Three-speed manual

Front suspension: . . . Coil springs, tube-type shock absorbers, stabilizer bar
Rear suspension: . . . Single transverse leaf spring, tube-type shock absorbers, independent with lateral struts
Axle ratio: 3.36:1
Frame: . . . . Steel box sections, welded

GENERAL:

Wheelbase, inches: 98
Track, front, inches: 56.8
rear, inches: 57.6
Brakes: . . . . Disc, four-wheel
Tire size, front and rear: 7.75-15
Wheels: . . . . Steel
Body material: . . . . Fiberglass
Assembly plant: . . . . St. Louis, Missouri

Production in 1966 reached the highest level of the 1963-67 series. There were 27,720 Corvettes made in 1966, of which 9,958 were coupes. Nineteen sixty-five production totaled 23,562 and just 8,186 were coupes. It was the lowest production year for coupes of the 1963-67 models.

Collectors view the 1965 as slightly more desirable than the 1966, but the difference is minimal, certainly nothing like the spread between 1963 and 1964 coupes. Value for both of these years is mainly determined by equipment and the option list for each year was immense.

Some are obvious winners. A 1965 with fuel-injection is a top-notch collector car and the awesome performance of the big-blocks make either year valuable if so equipped.

But no matter how equipped, all 1965 and 1966 Corvettes are potentially terrific cars. They are noticeably tighter than the previous Sting Rays, especially in convertible form. In fact, convertibles have enjoyed a new round of popularity since their demise in the mid-seventies, and Corvette enthusiasts consider the 1965-66 models (and 1967) great choices. Equipped with the removable hardtop and fold-down convertible top, they're three cars in one and drive like three different cars. Great fun.

The 1965 and 1966 Corvettes with big-block motors were distinguished by special hoods. Although the big-blocks added more weight where the Corvette least needed it, they are so unbelievably powerful that they can't help but be prized investment cars. But many have been badly abused. Exercise caution in purchasing one of these beasts. Wellington Morton photo.

1965 Corvette Colors/Options

Color Code	Body Color	Soft Top Color
AA	Tuxedo Black	Black/White/Beige
CC	Ermine White	Black/White/Beige
FF	Nassau Blue	Black/White/Beige
GG	Glen Green	Black/White/Beige
MM	Milano Maroon	Black/White/Beige
QQ	Silver Pearl	Black/White/Beige
UU	Rally Red	Black/White/Beige
XX	Goldwood Yellow	Black/White/Beige

INTERIOR COLORS: Black, Red, Blue, Saddle, Silver, White, Green, Maroon

Order #	Item Description	Sticker Price
19437	Base Corvette Sports Coupe	4321.00
19467	Base Corvette Convertible	4106.00
—	Genuine Leather Seat Trim	80.70
A01	Soft Ray Tinted Glass, All Windows	16.15
A02	Soft Ray Tinted Glass, Windshield	10.80
A31	Electric Power Windows	59.20
C07	Auxiliary Hardtop (for roadsters)	236.75
C48	Heater and Defroster Deletion (credit)	−100.00
C60	Air Conditioning	421.80
F40	Special Front and Rear Suspension	37.70
G81	Positraction Rear Axle, All Ratios	43.05
G91	Special Highway 3.08:1 Axle	2.20
J50	Power Brakes	43.05
J61	Drum Brake Substitution (credit)	−64.50
K66	Transistor Ignition System	75.35
L75	Optional 300 HP, 327 CI Engine	53.80
L76	Optional 365 HP, 327 CI Engine	129.15
L78	Optional 425 HP, 396 CI Engine	292.70
L79	Optional 350 HP, 327 CI Engine	107.60
L84	Optional 375 HP, 327 CI Engine (Fuel Inj)	538.00
M20	4-Speed Transmission	188.30
M22	4-Speed Close Ratio Transmission	236.95
M35	Powerglide Automatic Transmission	199.10
N03	36 Gallon Fuel Tank (coupe only)	202.30
N11	Off Road Exhaust System	37.70
N14	Side Mount Exhaust System	134.50
N32	Teakwood Steering Wheel	48.45
N36	Telescopic Steering Column	43.05
N40	Power Steering	96.85
P48	Special Cast Aluminum Knock-Off Wheels	322.80
P92	Whitewall Tires, 7.75x15	31.85
T01	Goldwall Tires, 7.75x15	50.05
U69	AM-FM Radio	203.40
Z01	Backup Lamps and Inside Day/Night Mirror	16.15

1966 Corvette Colors/Options

Color Code	Body Color	Soft Top Color
900	Tuxedo Black	Black/White/Beige
972	Ermine White	Black/White/Beige
976	Nassau Blue	Black/White/Beige
982	Mosport Green	Black/White/Beige
988	Milano Maroon	Black/White/Beige
986	Silver Pearl	Black/White/Beige
974	Rally Red	Black/White/Beige
984	Sunfire Yellow	Black/White/Beige
978	Laguna Blue	Black/White/Beige
980	Trophy Blue	Black/White/Beige

INTERIOR COLORS: Black, Red, Bright Blue, White-Blue, Silver, Saddle, Green, Blue

Order #	Item Description	Sticker Price
19437	Base Corvette Sport Coupe	4295.00
19467	Base Corvette Convertible	4084.00
—	Genuine Leather Seats	79.00
A01	Soft Ray Tinted Glass, All Windows	15.80
A02	Soft Ray Tinted Glass, Windshield	10.55
A31	Electric Power Windows	59.20
A82	Headrests	42.15
A85	Shoulder Harness	26.35
C07	Auxiliary Hardtop (for roadster)	231.75
C48	Heater and Defroster Deletion (credit)	−97.85
C60	Air Conditioning	412.90
F41	Special Front and Rear Suspension	36.90
G81	Positraction Rear Axle, All Ratios	42.15
J50	Power Brakes	43.05
J56	Special Heavy Duty Brakes	342.30
K66	Transistor Ignition System	73.75
L36	Optional 390 HP, 427 Engine	181.20
L72	Optional 450/425 HP, 427 CI Engine	312.85
L79	Optional 350 HP, 327 CI Engine	105.35
M20	4-Speed Transmission	184.30
M21	4-Speed Close Ratio Transmission	184.30
M22	4-Speed Close Ratio Transmission HD	237.00
M35	Powerglide Automatic Transmission	194.85
N03	36 Gallon Fuel Tank	198.05
N11	Off Road Exhaust System	36.90
N14	Side Mount Exhaust System	131.65
N32	Teakwood Steering Wheel	48.45
N36	Telescopic Steering Column	42.15
N40	Power Steering	94.80
P48	Special Cast Aluminum Knock-Off Wheels	326.00
P92	Whitewall Tires, 7.75x15	31.30
T01	Goldwall Tires, 7.75x15	46.55
U69	AM-FM Radio	199.10
V74	Traffic Hazard Lamp Switch	11.60

1966 Corvette 427 Coupe. Wellington Morton photo.

The side fender vents were made functional in 1965 and 1966. In both
years a side exhaust system was available. There was no muffler, just a
chambered pipe that wrapped from the engine down the sides of the
body. The outer surface was an aluminum heat shield. These systems
can be added to any 1963-67 model, but they were only factory available
from 1965-67. If you're contemplating adding side exhausts, ride in a
Corvette with them first. They are loud! And the acoustics of coupes
make side exhausts particularly irritating. But in a convertible with the
top down, there's nothing more exhilarating. Wellington Morton photo.

The knock-off aluminum wheel option continued in 1965 and 1966 but with small differences. Both were painted a flat gray-black between the fins. The 1965 had a bright center cone like the 1963 and 1964, but the cones of the 1966 had a brushed finish. Wellington Morton photo.

The door panels of the 1965 and 1966 models were a molded vinyl-on-foam design. They tended to crack along the sides of the armrest, but excellent reproductions are available today. The pull handle of the 1965 was plastic, colored to match the interior. Unfortunately, many pulled apart; the 1966 was metal as shown. The instrument layout of the 1965 and 1966 was the same as earlier Sting Rays, but the faces were flat, aircraft style. Beautiful. Wellington Morton photos.

CHAPTER 8
1967 CORVETTE

★★★★☆

★★★★★ (Big Block)

Serial Nos. 194677S100001 - 194677S122940*
(*for coupes, fourth digit is a 3)

The "mid-year" Corvettes are those built between 1963 and 1967, and often they're written about as a single group or series. Sometimes the mid-years are divided into two groups, 1963-64 and 1965-67. The logic most often cited is that the '65 and later cars should be segregated because disc brakes replaced drums in 1965.

But a lot of Corvette buffs group the 1967 model all by itself so I've done it here. To some of these folks, there are 1967's and there are the rest of 'em.

An analysis of mid-year selling prices will show the top prices are consistently paid for the 1963 and the 1967. The 1963 is understandable, but what's so special about the 1967?

First, understand that the 1967 is a Corvette that shouldn't even exist. Chevrolet had planned to put a new body on the Corvette chassis in 1967, but the new shape was delayed at the last minute by a year and finally arrived as the 1968 model. Chevrolet had to make do with the same old Sting Ray body for a fifth year. Stylists were told to change a few things, but time was short.

Normally, when this happens—change for the sake of change—the results are disastrous. But this time the opposite happened.

Rather than come up with new emblems and scripts, they just left most of them off. The 1967 is the cleanest, least adorned of any Sting Ray body.

Somebody in the government concluded that spinners on hubcaps and wheels posed a threat to society, so manufacturers were told to get them off their 1967 models. This meant the knock-off wheels optional on the 1963-66 Corvettes had to go. Chevrolet, possibly fearing the 1967 would turn out to be a slow seller since a new design was expected, decided to retool the aluminum wheel in a bolt-on style. This was particularly surprising because Chevrolet went to this expense for a wheel that would only be used for the 1967 Corvette. The 1968 was to use a wider rim to accommodate wider tires.

Again, a last minute redesign of a gorgeous wheel could be expected to yield dismal results, but it didn't. The 1967 bolt-on aluminum wheel was a masterpiece of exquisite detail and elegance. It was so nice, Corvette stylists dusted the design off and used a modified version on the 1982 Collector Edition.

Everything done to the 1967, the new side-fender louver treatment, the relocation of the handbrake from under the dash to between the seats, the new hood for 427-cubic-inch engines . . . everything came out right.

Demand did soften during 1967 and production dropped to 22,940, less than in either 1965 or 1966. Some feel the lighter schedule had a positive effect on quality. It's hard to say now, but the 1967 does get a lot of votes as the best-built Corvette ever.

1967 Corvette. Chevrolet photo.

It's rare to see a Corvette without a radio but this one didn't even have a heater. To discourage novice purchase of its L-88 engine option, a pure race machine sold to the public as a technicality to qualify it as a production vehicle, Chevrolet would not install radios or heaters. Bill Miller photo.

This was the L-88 engine, rated by Chevrolet at 430 horsepower, but actually having close to 600! Note the unusual air-cleaner-in-hood arrangement. Just 20 of the L-88 models were sold in 1967. Needless to say, these are very valuable today. Bill Miller photo.

Engines available in 1967, in addition to the standard 300-horsepower, 327-cubic-inch, included the 350-horsepower version of the 327, and three 427-cubic-inch variations rated at 390, 400 and 435 horsepower. Also, aluminum heads could be specified for the 435-horsepower mill for an extra $368.65. Oh, and there were a few other — twenty to be exact — 427 engine models sold to retail customers called L-88's.

Ah yes, the L-88. Rated at 430 horsepower, it had five less horsepower than the 435-horsepower L-71 engine. But at $947.90, the L-88 was more than twice as expensive. See, Chevrolet wasn't being exactly honest about the horsepower. The L-88 put out over 500, but the engine was intended expressly for racing and Chevrolet tried to discourage unknowing customers from ordering it by giving it a lower horsepower rating than the L-71.

A total of 216 L-88 Corvettes were retailed to customers in 1967, 1968 and 1969 models. But the twenty built in the 1967 model year qualifies them as the most rare. While these are very valuable collector cars, their usefulness is limited to just that, collecting. They were not intended for street use and no one should buy one with that in mind.

The 1967 is as close to a "can't lose" Corvette investment as you can get. The 1963-67 Corvette models have become the stars of the vintage Corvette group, and the 1967 has become the star of stars. It's the latest of the mid-years and with its many Corvette firsts — things like four-way flashers, dual master cylinders, turn signals with the lane-change feature added, six-inch rim widths, larger interior vent ports and folding seat back latches — the 1967 Corvette is thought by many to be the most refined Sting Ray of all. How many enthusiasts haven't heard about 1967 435-hp convertibles selling for Ferrari prices?

If Chevrolet had followed the 1967 Corvette with an even greater 1968 model, the 1967 would be thought of today as just another nice oldie. But the 1968 didn't turn out that way. A lot of potential new Corvette buyers in 1967 waited for the new body style coming in 1968. It was an understandable decision, but it looks now as if it wasn't the best one.

The GM Mark of Excellence sticker appeared in the door jamb of 1967 Corvettes. It was exclusive to the year. Author photo.

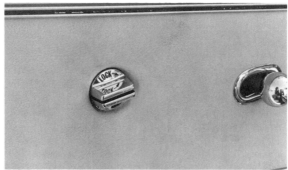

The handbrake moved to between the seats in 1967. Also, the inside door lock button moved forward several inches. Various reasons have been speculated for the move of the lock button, but the most likely is that it simply made it easier to reach. Author photos.

The side exhaust system introduced in 1965 continued to be available in 1967. But the backup light above the license plate was new and exclusive to the 1967 model. Author photos.

The 1967's instruments were similar to those of the previous two years, but 1967 did have the optional speed warning buzzer device pictured above. Author photo.

1967 Corvette Colors/Options

Color Code	Body Color	Soft Top Color
900	Tuxedo Black	Black/White/Teal Blue
972	Ermine White	Black/White/Teal Blue
980	Elkhart Blue	Black/White/Teal Blue
977	Lyndale Blue	Black/White/Teal Blue
976	Marina Blue	Black/White/Teal Blue
983	Goodwood Green	Black/White/Teal Blue
974	Rally Red	Black/White/Teal Blue
986	Silver Pearl	Black/White/Teal Blue
984	Sunfire Yellow	Black/White/Teal Blue
988	Marlboro Maroon	Black/White/Teal Blue

INTERIOR COLORS: Black, Red, Bright Blue, Saddle, White-Blue, White-Black, Teal Blue, Green

Order #	Item Description	Sticker Price
19437	Base Corvette Sport Coupe	$4388.75
19467	Base Corvette Convertible	4240.75
—	Genuine Leather Seats	79.00
A01	Soft Ray Tinted Glass, All Windows	15.80
A02	Soft Ray Tinted Glass, Windshield	10.55
A31	Electric Power Windows	57.95
A82	Headrests	42.15
A85	Shoulder Belts (coupe only)	26.35
C07	Auxiliary Hardtop (for roadster)	231.75
C08	Vinyl Covering for Auxiliary Hardtop	52.70
C48	Heater and Defroster Deletion (credit)	−97.85
C60	Air Conditioning	412.90
F41	Special Front and Rear Suspension	36.90
J50	Power Brakes	42.15
J56	Special Heavy Duty Brakes	342.30
K66	Transistor Ignition System	73.75
L36	Optional 390 HP, 427 CI Engine	200.15
L68	Optional 400 HP, 427 CI Engine	305.50
L71	Optional 435 HP, 427 CI Engine	437.10
L79	Optional 350 HP, 327 CI Engine	105.35
L88	Optional 430 HP, 427 CI Engine	947.90
L89	Aluminum Cylinder Heads for L71	368.65
M20	4-Speed Transmission	184.35
M21	4-Speed Close Ratio Transmission	184.35
M22	4-Speed Close Ratio Transmission HD	237.00
M35	Powerglide Automatic Transmission	194.35
N03	36 Gallon Fuel Tank (coupe only)	198.05
N11	Off Road Exhaust System	36.90
N14	Side Mount Exhaust System	131.65
N36	Telescopic Steering Column	42.15
N40	Power Steering	94.80
N89	Special Cast Aluminum Bolt-On Wheels	263.30
P92	Whitewall Tires, 7.75x15	31.35
QB1	Redline Tires, 7.75x15	46.65
U15	Speed Warning Indicator	10.55
U69	AM-FM Radio	172.75

The 1967 Corvette was one of the first to show signs of federal input in the area of safety. One such result in 1967 was a flatter design for the control knobs. Author photo.

As if 427 cubic inches weren't enough, in 1967 you could even get a 3x2 carburetor setup with either 400 or 435 horsepower. This arrangement was characterized by the unusual triangular air cleaner. The distinctive hood was unique to 1967 models with the 427 motors. Author photos.

The "rally" wheel was standard fare in 1967. Federal law mandated the removal of spinners from wheels in 1967 so the knock-off wheel of 1963-66 was replaced with the "bolt-on" in 1967. The center cone of this gorgeous wheel pried off to reveal lug nuts. Like the knock-offs, the popularity of this wheel has resulted in reproductions, but originals are detectible and far more valuable. Bill Miller and author photos.

1967 Corvette

BASE ENGINE

Type: . . . . .Chevrolet ohv V-8
Bore x stroke, inches: . . . . .4.00 x 3.25
Displacement, inches: 327
Compression ratio:. 10.25:1
Carburetion:. . . . . .Single four-barrel carburetor
Horsepower:. 300
Distributor: . . . . .Single point breaker
Other engines offered:. . .Higher horsepower variations were
    available in both 1965 and 1966. See option charts.

CHASSIS AND DRIVETRAIN

Clutch:. . . . . .Single dry-plate
Transmission:. . . . . .Three-speed manual

Front suspension:. . .Coil springs, tube-type shock absorbers,
    stabilizer bar
Rear suspension:. . .Single transverse leaf spring, tube-type
    shock absorbers, independent with lateral struts
Axle ratio: 3.36:1
Frame: .Steel box sections, welded

GENERAL:

Wheelbase, inches: 98
Track, front, inches: 57.6
    rear, inches: 58.3
Brakes:. . . . . .Disc, four-wheel
Tire size, front and rear: .7.75-15
Wheels: . . . . .Steel
Body material: . . . . .Fiberglass
Assembly plant: . . . . .St. Louis, Missouri

 (Big Block)

Serial Nos. 1968: 194678S400001 - 194678S428566*
1969: 194679S700001 - 194679S738762*
(*for coupes, fourth digit is a 3)

The 1968 Corvette was restyled with a new body shape; a toned-down version of the Mako Shark-inspired design originally planned for introduction as the 1967 model. The new shape was lower, slightly wider and more aerodynamic. No one realized it at the time, but the Corvette wouldn't see another complete body change until the 1984 model, a full fifteen years later.

Magazine journalists have always found it difficult to accept anything American built as a "real sports car," whatever that means. And Corvette fit and finish was always open to some complaints. But Corvettes built in the mid-sixties, especially the 1965-67 models, were very well designed and constructed cars and didn't offer anything really juicy for the critics. This changed in 1968. The critics had a field day.

Part of the negative press reaction to the 1968 Corvette was design related. Few could argue the car didn't look good, "dramatic" being a favorite adjective. But the new design required compromises. The body was a little wider at its widest point, but the "Coke-bottle" shape and a transmission tunnel made bigger to accommodate the three-speed automatics created a cabin that was noticeably cramped. Some called it cave-like.

To accommodate the lower roofline, seat backs were raked at thirty-three degrees compared to twenty-five degrees the year before. The seats had little support of any kind and a sliding-board effect caused occupants to have to constantly reposition themselves. Side vent windows were eliminated and the window-to-seat relationship was such that driving with an elbow out the window was uncomfortable at best. The doors didn't close with the reassuring "thunk" purists preferred, but rather with a crash of internal rattles.

Starting with the doors, the 1968 Corvette's real problem lay in a perceived lack of quality control. Magazine reviews, particularly one by *Car and Driver*, literally roasted Chevrolet for building a piece of junk. *Car and Driver* recited a litany of quality ailments and proclaimed its test Corvette too shabby to merit testing. The *Car and Driver* road test—actually, the lack of it—sent shock waves through General Motors.

Reviews of this sort can have enormous impact on a new car and its reputation. Some of the *Car and Driver* criticisms pointed out real problems that required design attention and correction. Most were of a nuisance nature, things a fairly competent owner could correct in a weekend. So someone looking at the car now as a restoration candidate isn't too concerned, but the new-car buyer in 1968

No one could deny the beauty of 1968 styling; the shape was good enough to last fifteen years. But the 1968 met a barrage of criticism for quality problems and design glitches. It has never recovered, but watch this one—it could be a sleeper. Note that the side exhaust system shown has been owner-added. This side exhaust style was a factory option, but only in 1969. Author photo.

The body sides of the 1968 and 1969 models wrapped under the tires, ex-
posing painted surfaces to debris thrown by the extra-wide rubber. The
side exhaust style shown was available only in 1969. Author photo.

certainly was turned off. The 1968 Corvette got saddled early with the reputation of being a quality disaster, and it has never shaken that reputation to this day.

The magazine criticism of the 1968 Corvette did wake Chevrolet up and serve it notice that the Corvette market couldn't be taken for granted. The Corvette had already attracted a tremendous following, a momentum a couple of bad reviews couldn't halt. But Chevrolet realized the Corvette couldn't rest on its laurels for long.

Quality problems were attacked and reduced, and components were redesigned to make the car more livable. One example was a quick redesign of the inner door panels to get more desperately needed shoulder room in the cramped cockpit.

Chevrolet stopped calling its Corvette the Sting Ray in 1968 but thought better of it and put the name back on in 1969. A subtle point, but the 1963-67 Corvettes were Sting Rays (two words), whereas the 1969 was a Stingray. The body styling of both the 1968 and 1969 was identical other than details like the Stingray script on the side fenders of the latter. Other details included a different type of exterior door opener. The 1968 had a thumb button and a finger depression plate above it. The button was removed in 1969 and the depression plate triggered the door mechanism. Also, the 1968 had separate backup lights placed under the bumpers whereas the 1969 had them incorporated into the regular taillights.

Nineteen sixty-eight Corvettes had the ignition switch on the dash, but it moved to the steering column in 1969. The cutaway dash design left no room for a glovebox in the normal location in the 1968, but at least the 1969 got some map pockets.

The 1968 and 1969 Corvettes retained hidden headlights but the units were vacuum-operated rather than electrically. The vacuum units moved the lights into driving position more quickly and have proven to be very trouble-free. The hidden headlights of Corvettes were vacuum-operated through 1982.

But the 1968 and 1969 Corvettes also had a vacuum-operated lid which covered the windshield wipers when not in use. The lid was a styling gimmick borrowed from the Mako Shark dream car. Its tendency to malfunction was one of the items that tarnished the quality image of these cars. I remember that the lid of my own 1969 would pop up whenever it felt like it, then crunch down on the wiper arms when the wiper switch was turned on. Also, some owners have complained about the lid icing over, but my own experience was that the lid mechanism was powerful enough to crack through anything an Ohio winter could produce.

Both coupe and convertible body styles continued in 1968, but the coupe was a different breed than before. It was a "T" top with two removable roof panels and a rear window which could also be removed. Both years and body styles had a fiber-optics light-monitoring system with a display panel on the center console.

Wheel width in 1968 increased from six inches to seven, an increase made possible by the body's redesign to accommodate wider tires. Rim width increased again, to eight inches, in 1969. But the steering-wheel diameter was reduced from sixteen inches in the 1968 to fifteen in the 1969.

Stereo radios could be ordered on both years, but the side-mount exhaust systems were available only in 1969.

The quality problems associated with the 1968 and, to a lesser degree, the 1969 have obviously tarnished these models. Collectors don't hold them in great esteem but this very fact has kept prices reasonable. There has always been a small band of Corvette enthusiasts who draw an analogy between the 1963 and 1968 models and assume that 1968's will eventually explode in value.

Anything's possible, but the analogy falls apart under scrutiny. The 1963 Corvette was widely praised from its first introductory day and led a procession of wildly popular cars. The 1968 was tainted from day one. It did lead off a fifteen-year Corvette series, but those were years of much higher volume than the four that followed 1963.

Both big- and small-blocks continued in 1968 and 1969. The big engines for both years were still 427 cubic inches, but the small-blocks went from 327 cubic inches in 1968 to 350 in 1969. Government-mandated emission devices were starting to creep in, but blistering performance packages could be ordered in both years. In 1968 and 1969, the L-88 version of the 427 was available. This was a pure racing engine capable of over 500 horsepower. It was sold quietly to the public to qualify it as a "production" vehicle.

In 1969, Chevrolet offered another engine that had no business in a street car, the ZL-1. This one also pumped out over 500 horsepower, but was aluminum for weight savings. The ZL-1 option was a racing package consisting of the engine and suspension components. The option cost was $3,000, which seemed outrageous but really wasn't. Though ZL-1 parts found their way out of Chevrolet Engineering to the racetracks, official records show that only two ZL-1-optioned 1969 Corvettes were delivered to retail customers.

These thundering engines available from the factory prompted John Greenwood, the famous Corvette road racer, to comment in a recent interview that the 1968-69 Corvettes were his personal favorites because they were so nearly race-ready right off the show room floor.

While these racing engines make for great conversation—imagine driving away from your local Chevy dealer in a bone-stock automobile capable of speeds in excess of 170 mph—they're for serious drivers and collectors only. Corvettes equipped with these engines are practically useless for street driving. To discourage anything but race customers, Chevrolet wouldn't even install heaters in L-88 or ZL-1 Corvettes. These cars were offered to the public only as a technicality necessary to qualify them as "production" race vehicles.

The body of the 1968-69 was wrapped under the wheels so that rocks thrown by the tires chipped the lower body sides. Without a doubt, the big tires hanging out from the body gave these models a very hairy business-only look. But the body was altered the following year to solve the chip problem.

Despite a slow start, production of the 1968 Corvette jumped to 28,566, a new Corvette record. Strikes stalled the start of 1969 production, so when things finally got rolling Chevrolet decided to just let them roll. Nineteen sixty-nine production went four months into the 1970 production schedule and resulted in a whopping 38,762 1969's built.

Corvette buffs rate the 1968 and 1969 models about equally in desirability, with the 1968 having perhaps a small edge. It has the advantage of lower production, it was the first of the series, and it has several unique features collectors look for. The 1969 is less unique and more plentiful but has a better quality image. As a restoration candidate, the 1968 is preferred by some for the reasons listed and because the quality problems associated with fit and finish can be corrected during refurbishing.

Unique features of the 1968 included a push-button door release and a dash-mounted ignition switch. In the 1969, the depression plate in the door activated the door mechanism and the ignition switch moved to the steering column. Author photos.

The 1968 introduced a new interior with seats raked at 33 degrees, the most severe in Corvette's history. Author photo.

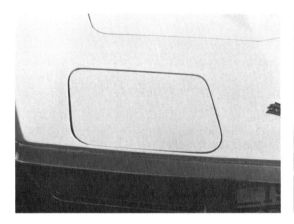

Hidden headlights continued with the 1968 model, but these popped up instead of revolving into position. Also, these and all subsequent Corvette headlight units through 1982 were vacuum-operated rather than electrically. Author photos.

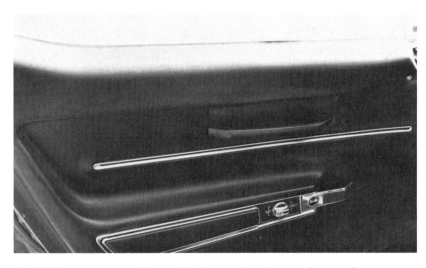

The 1968 inner door panel (late style shown above) was unique to the year with a horizontal pull handle and a thick upper section that limited shoulder room. The 1969 panel (right) used a vertical pull and a thinner section in the shoulder area. Author photos.

The 1968 model introduced a number of styling touches, some of which didn't work out well in service. One was this vacuum-operated lid, which covered the windshield wipers when not in use. The lid's vacuum action tended to be a little unpredictable and icing could cause difficulty. Author photo.

The Stingray name was not used on the 1968 Corvette, but returned in 1969. The trim liners for the side fender slots were optional only in 1969. Author photo.

1968 Corvette Colors/Options

Color Code	Body Color	Soft Top Color
900	Tuxedo Black	Black/White/Beige
972	Polar White	Black/White/Beige
992	Corvette Bronze	Black/White/Beige
976	LeMans Blue	Black/White/Beige
978	International Blue	Black/White/Beige
988	Cordovan Maroon	Black/White/Beige
974	Rally Red	Black/White/Beige
986	Silverstone Silver	Black/White/Beige
983	British Green	Black/White/Beige
984	Safari Yellow	Black/White/Beige

INTERIOR COLORS: Black, Red, Medium Blue, Dark Blue, Dark Orange, Tobacco, Gunmetal

Order #	Item Description	Sticker Price
19437	Base Corvette Sport Coupe	4663.00
19467	Base Corvette Convertible	4320.00
—	Genuine Leather Seat Trim	79.00
A01	Soft Ray Tinted Glass, All Windows	15.80
A31	Electric Power Windows	57.95
A82	Head Restraints	42.15
A85	Custom Shoulder Belts	26.35
C07	Auxiliary Hardtop (for roadster)	231.75
C08	Vinyl Covering For Auxiliary Hardtop	52.70
C50	Rear Window Defroster	31.60
C60	Air Conditioning	412.90
F41	Special Front and Rear Suspension	36.90
G81	Positraction Rear Axle, All Ratios	46.35
J50	Power Brakes	42.15
J56	Heavy Duty Breaks	384.45
K66	Transistor Ignition System	73.75
L36	Optional 390 HP, 427 CI Engine	200.15
L68	Optional 400 HP, 427 CI Engine	305.50
L71	Optional 435 HP, 427 CI Engine	437.10
L79	Optional 350 HP, 327 CI Engine	105.35
L88	Optional 435 HP, 427 CI Engine	947.90
L71/81	Optional 435 HP, 427 CI Engine	805.75
M20	4-Speed Transmission	184.35
M21	4-Speed Close Ratio Transmission	184.35
M22	4-Speed Close Ratio Transmission HD	263.30
M40	Turbo-Hydramatic Transmission	226.45
N11	Off Road Exhaust System	36.90
N36	Telescopic Steering Column	42.15
N40	Power Steering	94.80
P01	Bright Metal Wheel Cover	57.95
PT6	Red Stripe Nylon Tires, F70x15	31.30
PT7	White Stripe Nylon Tires, F70x15	31.30
UA6	Alarm System	26.35
U15	Speed Warning Indicator	10.55
U69	AM-FM Radio	172.75
U79	AM-FM Stereo Radio	278.10

1969 Corvette Colors/Options

Color Code	Body Color	Soft Top Color
900	Tuxedo Black	Black/White/Beige
972	Can-Am White	Black/White/Beige
974	Monza Red	Black/White/Beige
976	LeMans Blue	Black/White/Beige
990	Monaco Orange	Black/White/Beige
983	Fathom Green	Black/White/Beige
984	Daytona Yellow	Black/White/Beige
986	Cortez Silver	Black/White/Beige
988	Burgundy	Black/White/Beige
980	Riverside Gold	Black/White/Beige

INTERIOR COLORS: Black, Bright Blue, Green, Red, Gunmetal, Saddle

Order #	Item Description	Sticker Price
19437	Base Corvette Sport Coupe	$4780.95
19467	Base Corvette Convertible	4437.95
—	Genuine Leather Seat Trim	79.00
A01	Soft Ray Tinted Glass, All Windows	16.90
A31	Electric Power Windows	63.20
A85	Custom Shoulder Belts	42.15
C07	Auxiliary Hardtop (for roadster)	252.80
C08	Vinyl Covering for Auxiliary Hardtop	57.95
C50	Rear Window Defroster	32.65
C60	Air Conditioning	428.70
F41	Special Front and Rear Suspension	36.90
—	Positraction Rear Axle, All Ratios	46.35
J50	Power Brakes	42.15
K05	Engine Block Heater	10.55
K66	Transistor Ignition System	81.10
L36	Optional 390 HP, 427 CI Engine	221.20
L46	Optional 350 HP, 350 CI Engine	131.65
L68	Optional 400 HP, 427 CI Engine	326.55
L71	Optional 435 HP, 427 CI Engine	437.10
L88	Optional 435 HP, 427 CI Engine	1032.15
L89	Optional 435 HP, 427 CI Engine	832.05
ZL1	Optional Special 427 CI Engine	3000.00
M20	4-Speed Transmission	184.80
M21	4-Speed Close Ratio Transmission	184.80
M22	4-Speed Close Ratio Transmission Heavy Duty	290.40
M40	Turbo Hydramatic Transmission	221.80
N14	Side Mount Exhaust System	147.45
N37	Tilt-Telescopic Steering Column	84.30
N40	Power Steering	105.35
P02	Wheel Covers	57.95
PT6/PT7	Red Stripe/White Stripe Nylon Tires	31.30
TJ2	Front Fender Louver Trim	21.10
UA6	Alarm System	26.35
U15	Speed Warning Indicator	11.60
U69	AM-FM Radio	172.45
U79	AM-FM Stereo Radio	278.10

1969 Corvette convertible. Author photo.

1968-1969 Corvette

BASE ENGINE

Type: . . . . .Chevrolet ohv V-8
Bore x stroke, inches: 4.00 x 3.25 (1968). 4.00 x 3.48 (1969)
Displacement, inches: 327 (1968), 350 (1969)
Compression ratio:. 10.25:1
Carburetion:. . . . . .Single four-barrel carburetor
Horsepower:. 300
Distributor: . . . . .Single point breaker
Other engines offered:. . .Higher horsepower variations were
    available in both 1968 and 1969. See option charts.

CHASSIS AND DRIVETRAIN

Clutch:. . . . . .Single dry-plate
Transmission:. . . . . .Three-speed manual

Front suspension:. . .Coil springs, tube-type shock absorbers,
    stabilizer bar
Rear suspension:. . .Single transverse leaf spring, tube-type
    shock absorbers, independent with lateral struts
Axle ratio: 3.36:1
Frame: .Steel box sections, welded

GENERAL:

Wheelbase, inches: 98
Track, front, inches: 58.3 (1968), 58.7 (1969)
    rear, inches: 59.0 (1968), 59.4 (1969)
Brakes:. . . . . .Disc, four-wheel
Tire size, front and rear: F70-15
Wheels: . . . . .Steel
Body material: . . . . .Fiberglass
Assembly plant: . . . . .St. Louis, Missouri

CHAPTER 10
1970-1972 CORVETTE

(Big Block)
(LT1)

Serial Nos. 1970: 194670S400001 - 194670S417316*
1971: 194671S100001 - 194671S121801*
1972: 1Z67K2S500001 - 1Z67K2S527004**
(*for coupes, fourth digit is a 3)
(**for coupes, third digit is a 3. Fifth
digit varies with engine installed)

The seventies saw a tremendous evolution occur in the Corvette. When introduced in 1953, it was aimed at the country club crowd. Zora Arkus-Duntov guided it into a performance image where all else was secondary. As government mandates forced their way into the industry, the Corvette changed again. This time it turned into a more sedate but luxurious personal touring machine. It went from street scorcher to gran turisimo. The evolution went quite smoothly even though the Beach Boys did stop singing about it.

The engine option list was shortened in 1970 but strong versions of the small-block 350-cubic-inch engines and a new 454-cubic-inch engine were available. One factor making 1970 Corvettes so desirable to many is that it was the last year of high-compression engines. Compression went down the following year to permit burning lower octane fuels so the oil companies could start phasing in low- and no-lead fuels at their stations before the advent of catalytic converters.

In 1970, Chevrolet introduced a new engine for the Corvette called the LT-1, and it turned out to be a honey! It was a solid-lifter version of the 350-cubic-inch engine and developed 370 horsepower. The Corvette hadn't had anything like it since 1965.

The 1970 got a very late production start due to an extra long 1969 model run. There were 17,316 Corvettes built in 1970 compared to 21,801 in 1971. Other than a few color changes and a switch to amber turn-signal lenses early in 1971 production, the two models were virtual duplicates. Something did end in 1971. It was the last year for the fiber-optics light-monitoring system.

A lot ended in 1972. Fewer engine varieties were available and power ratings went down. The drop in horsepower was due to terminology, a change from gross ratings to net ratings, as-installed figures which included the losses from the fan, air cleaners, mufflers and the like.

The 1972 was the last Corvette to have a removable rear window. This deletion went pretty much unnoticed at the time, but it's interesting to note that the original concept for the '68 body style was for a single "targa" type of roof panel combined with the removable window. As originally planned, this would have yielded a coupe with a much airier feel than the center support design, which was

The 1970 Corvette had the reputation of being a vastly improved model. Additions included square exhaust ports and flared wheel wells to solve the tire debris problems of the 1968-69 models. The 1970 was also the last Corvette with high-compression engines. Chevrolet photo.

Front turn lamps were redesigned in 1970 and the grille texture was new.
Chevrolet photo.

dictated by the lack of a storage area large enough to accommodate the single removable panel. But in their first production form, the "T" top coupes did at least keep the removable rear window concept. In 1973, even it was gone.

The 1972 was the last Corvette with conventional chrome bumpers at both ends. It was the last with the hidden windshield wiper feature and the last with a metal egg-crate grille. It was the last year for the LT-1 engine and the only year the popular engine could be combined with air conditioning.

Today, the 1970 Corvette is a popular year. Problems with the preceding two years were mostly sorted out, yet the 1970 still had the high-compression engines including the new LT-1. And production of the 1970 was the lowest since 1962.

Nineteen seventy-one is viewed less favorably, mainly because of the switch to lower compression. In truth, the performance differential is negligible in everyday driving and the compression change permits using the lower octane fuels that are common today.

The 1972 has emerged as another Corvette "keeper." This takes some explaining since it was nearly the same as the 1971 model. What apparently happens in enthusiasts' minds is that the 1970 and 1971 get lumped together and the 1970 wins because of its stronger engines. The 1972 gets separate consideration. Since so much ended with the 1972 model, it seems to get the nostalgia vote.

A real favorite is the 1972 equipped with LT-1 engine and air conditioning. This is a combination Chevrolet didn't particularly like to offer. The problem is that the LT-1 has solid lifters, which permit higher rpm; and higher revolutions spin air-conditioning belts off their pulleys. Some of the mid-year Corvettes got the solid lifter/air conditioning combination, but not many. According to *Corvette News,* a mere 240 of the 1972 models were so equipped, though some sources place the number slightly higher.

1970-1971-1972 Corvette

BASE ENGINE

Type: . . . . .Chevrolet ohv V-8
Bore x stroke, inches: .4.00 x 3.48
Displacement, inches: 350
Compression ratio: 10.25:1 (1970), 8.5:1 (1971, 1972)
Carburetion:. . . . . .Single four-barrel carburetor
Horsepower: 300 (1970), 270 (1971), 200 (1972)
Distributor: .Single point breaker
Other engines offered:...Higher horsepower variations were available in 1970, 1971 and 1972. See option charts.

CHASSIS AND DRIVETRAIN

Clutch: . . . . .Single dry-plate (manual)
Transmission:. . Four-speed manual or three-speed automatic

Front suspension:...Coil springs, tube-type shock absorbers, stabilizer bar
Rear suspension:...Single transverse leaf spring, tube-type shock absorbers, independent with lateral struts
Axle ratio: . . . . .3.36:1 (manual), 3.08:1 (automatic)
Frame: . . . . .Steel box sections, welded

GENERAL:

Wheelbase, inches: 98
Track, front, inches: 58.7
rear, inches: 59.4
Brakes:. . . . . .Disc, four-wheel
Tire size, front and rear: F70-15
Wheels: . . . . .Steel
Body material: . . . . .Fiberglass
Assembly plant: . . . . .St. Louis, Missouri

The 1970-72 Corvettes were the last to feature chrome bumpers front and rear. In 1973, the front bumper changed to body-colored flexible plastic. In 1974, the rear followed suit. Author photos.

1970 Corvette Colors/Options

Color Code	Body Color	Soft Top Color
976	Mulsanne Blue	Black/White
979	Birdgehampton Blue	Black/White
982	Donnybrooke Green	Black/White
992	Laguna Gray	Black/White
975	Marlboro Maroon	Black/White
993	Corvette Bronze	Black/White
974	Monza Red	Black/White
986	Cortez Silver	Black/White
972	Classic White	Black/White
984	Daytona Yellow	Black/White

INTERIOR COLORS: Black, Blue, Brown, Red, Green, Saddle

Order #	Item Description	Sticker Price
19437	Base Corvette Sport Coupe	5192.00
19467	Base Corvette Convertible	4849.00
—	Custom Interior Trim	158.00
A31	Electric Power Windows	63.20
A85	Custom Shoulder Belts	42.15
C07	Auxiliary Hardtop (for roadster)	273.85
C08	Vinyl Covering for Auxiliary Hardtop	63.20
C50	Rear Window Defroster	36.90
C60	Air Conditioning	447.65
—	Positraction Axle, Optional Ratio	12.65
J50	Power Brakes	47.40
L46	Optional 350 HP, 350 CI Engine	158.00
LS5	Optional 390 HP, 454 CI Engine	289.65
LT1	Optional 370 HP, 350 CI Engine	447.60
M21	4-Speed Close Ratio Transmission	nc
M22	4-Speed Close Ratio Transmission Heavy Duty	95.00
M40	Turbo Hydramatic Transmission	nc
N37	Tilt-Telescopic Steering Column	84.30
N40	Power Steering	105.35
P01	Custom Wheel Covers	57.95
PT7	White Stripe Nylon Tires, F70x15	31.30
PU9	White Letter Nylon Tires, F70x15	33.15
T60	Heavy Duty Battery	15.80
UA6	Alarm System	31.60
U69	AM-FM Radio	172.75
U79	AM-FM Stereo Radio	278.10

1971 Corvette Colors/Options

Color Code	Body Color	Soft Top Color
976	Mulsanne Blue	Black/White
979	Birdgehampton Blue	Black/White
983	Brands Hatch Green	Black/White
988	Steel Cities Gray	Black/White
987	Ontario Orange	Black/White
973	Mille Miglia Red	Black/White
905	Nevada Silver	Black/White
972	Classic White	Black/White
912	Sunflower Yellow	Black/White
989	War Bonnet Yellow	Black/White

INTERIOR COLORS: Black, Dark Blue, Dark Green, Red, Saddle

Order #	Item Description	Sticker Price
19437	Base Corvette Sport Coupe	5496.00
19467	Base Corvette Convertible	5259.00
—	Custom Interior Trim	158.00
A31	Electric Power Windows	79.00
A85	Custom Shoulder Belts	42.00
C07	Auxiliary Hardtop (for roadster)	274.00
C08	Vinyl Covering for Auxiliary Hardtop	63.00
C50	Rear Window Defroster	42.00
C60	Air Conditioning	459.00
—	Positraction Axle, Optional Ratio	13.00
J50	Power Brakes	47.00
LS5	Optional 365 HP, 454 CI Engine	295.00
LS6	Optional 425 HP, 454 CI Engine	1221.00
LT1	Optional 330 HP, 350 CI Engine	483.00
ZR1	Optional 330 HP, 350 CI Engine	1010.00
ZR2	Optional 425 HP, 454 CI Engine	1747.00
M21	4-Speed Close Ratio Transmission	nc
M22	4-Speed Close Ratio Transmission Heavy Duty	100.00
M40	Turbo Hydramatic Transmission	nc
N37	Tilt-Telescopic Steering Column	84.30
N40	Power Steering	115.90
P02	Wheel Covers	63.00
PT7	White Stripe Nylon Tires, F70x15	28.00
PU9	White Lettered Nylon Tires, F70x15	42.00
T60	Heavy Duty Battery	15.80
U69	AM-FM Radio	178.00
U79	AM-FM Stereo Radio	283.00

A lot ended for the Corvette in 1972. This was the last Corvette to have a removable rear window (coupes), and the last to have a solid-lifter engine available. The car shown had the particularly nice combination of an LT-1 engine and air conditioning. Author photos.

This beautiful side fender grille treatment was exclusive to the 1970, 1971 and 1972 models. Author photo.

The hidden wiper treatment was used on the 1970-72 Corvettes, but 1972 was the last year. In the down position, the door nicely hides the wipers, but the mechanism proved somewhat troublesome for everyday use. Author photos.

At left is the release button for the removable rear window, a feature that ceased with the 1972 model. The buttons and knob under the steering column were manual overrides for the vacuum-operated headlight units and windshield wiper lid. Author photos.

Chevrolet dropped solid-lifter engines from the Corvette lineup in 1966, but enthusiasts weren't happy about it. In 1970, a new solid-lifter engine called the LT-1 became available and was a real favorite. This engine was available only during the 1970-72 period and was characterized by a distinctive hood (1972 shown). Author photo.

Cast aluminum wheels were not available in the 1968-72 period, but this finely detailed wheel disc was optional. Author photo.

1972 Corvette Colors/Options

Color Code	Body Color	Soft Top Color
945	Bryar Blue	Black/White
979	Targa Blue	Black/White
988	Steel Cities Gray	Black/White
946	Elkhart Green	Black/White
987	Ontario Orange	Black/White
973	Mille Miglia Red	Black/White
924	Pewter Silver	Black/White
972	Classic White	Black/White
912	Sunflower Yellow	Black/White
989	War Bonnet Yellow	Black/White

INTERIOR COLORS: Black, Blue, Red, Saddle

Order #	Item Description	Sticker Price
19437	Base Corvette Sport Coupe	5533.00
19467	Base Corvette Convertible	5296.00
—	Custom Interior Trim	158.00
A31	Electric Power Windows	85.35
A85	Custom Shoulder Belts	26.35
C07	Auxiliary Hardtop (for roadster)	273.85
C08	Vinyl Roof Covering For Auxiliary Hardtop	158.00
C50	Rear Window Defroster	42.15
C60	Air Conditioning	464.50
—	Positraction Axle, Optional Ratio	12.65
J50	Power Brakes	47.40
LS5	Optional 270 HP, 454 CI Engine	294.90
LT1	Optional 255 HP, 350 CI Engine	483.45
ZR1	Optional 255 HP, 350 CI Engine	1010.05
M21	4-Speed Close Ratio Transmission	nc
M40	Turbo Hydramatic Transmission	nc
N37	Tilt-Telescopic Steering Column	84.30
N40	Power Steering	115.90
P02	Custom Wheel Covers	63.20
PT7	White Stripe Nylon Tires, F70x15	30.35
PU9	White Lettered Nylon Tires, F70x15	43.65
T60	Heavy Duty Battery	15.80
U69	AM-FM Radio	178.00
U79	AM-FM Stereo Radio	283.35

CHAPTER 11
1973-1977 CORVETTE

✪✪
✪✪◖ (Big Block)
✪✪✪ (1975 Convertible)

Serial Nos. 1973: 1Z67J3S400001 - 1Z67J3S434464*
 1974: 1Z67J4S400001 - 1Z67J4S437502*
 1975: 1Z67J5S400001 - 1Z67J5S438465*
 1976: 1Z37L6S400001 - 1Z37L6S446558
 1977: 1Z37L7S400001 - 1Z37L7S449213
 (*for coupes, third digit is a 3)
 (fifth digit in all serial numbers varies
 with engine installed)

Corvettes got heavier and slower during the years from 1973 to 1977. The option list shrank and by 1977 optional engine choices were down to one. The body didn't change much and after 1975 wasn't even available in convertible configuration.

Yet during this period Chevrolet built and sold 202,202 Corvettes, more than any previous five-year period, almost more than all previous Corvette models combined.

The reason is that every other company wishing to sell its products in the United States faced the same federal mandates that Chevrolet did. The Corvettes of the period may have been overshadowed by earlier Corvettes, but Corvette's competitors were in the same pollution control soup and the Corvette more than held its own. There were always better cars to be had. But "for the money," always the great equalizer in the Corvette's favor, kept Chevy's two-seater in its premier position. You can't attribute the Corvette's success during 1973-77 merely to its rich heritage. Chevrolet's engineers coped with and met the challenges of the day as well as any competition, what little there was.

This isn't to say that nothing significant happened during the period. The 1973 got a new hood, designed around the elimination of the troublesome hidden wiper setup. Its front bumper was body-colored, designed to meet federal 5-mph crash standards, but the rear remained the same as the previous year. Engineers were determined to make the 1973 quieter and changed the chassis mounts to isolate road noise more effectively. Also, sound-deadening material was sprayed on selected inner panels and a pad was added to the inner hood.

The 1974 was the first to have body-colored bumper treatment both front and rear. It was the last with a real dual exhaust, non-catalytic converter system. It was the last with the 454-cubic-inch engine on the option list. Even though the engines were all weaker, the 454 still propelled the 1974 Corvette in a most exciting manner.

Nineteen seventy-five was the year of the catalytic converter, not a wonderful distinction. It was the first for standard electronic (point-less distributor) ignitions and bladder-style fuel cell. But the 1975's real claim to fame is that it was

The 1973 Corvette was the only one with the soft body-colored nose and abrupt rear with chrome bumpers. Larry Shinoda, the famous Corvette designer, once commented in an interview that the 1973 was his favorite of the post-1967 era because the front and rear styling were closest to what the stylists originally had in mind when this series was first designed. The aluminum wheels shown in this photo were offered briefly in 1973, then canceled due to strength problems. They kept reappearing on the option sheets, but weren't actually available again until 1976. Author photo.

the year the convertible was phased out. Everyone concluded right away that the 1975 convertible was sure to be a collector piece. It is, but the lofty prices some had predicted haven't materialized.

The 1976 set a new production record of 46,558. This had more to do with a strong market in general than any new innovations. Aluminum wheels became optional, a maintenance-free battery was added, and a new "sport steering wheel" borrowed from the Vega was added. Hardly the things enthusiasts dream about.

Things started perking up in 1977. Major changes were in the works for 1978, the Corvette's silver anniversary, and stylists allowed a few of the new things to trickle into the 1977. The center console was a new design that included a deeper radio slot to accept standard Delco radios. This was good, since it allowed the full line of Delco products to be made available in the Corvette. Previously, the need for a unique Corvette radio and the Corvette's relatively low volume meant a limited radio choice. Nobody seemed to notice that the style of the new console didn't match the rest of the interior too well. The rest was coming the following year.

In 1977, cruise control became optional for the first time, but only with automatic transmissions. The headlight dimmer, windshield wiper and washer controls all moved to the directional-signal stalk.

With the possible exception of models like the 1975 convertible and 1974 with 454-cubic-inch motor, Corvettes built in the 1973-77 period can never be seriously considered as collector cars. That doesn't mean some won't hold their value well or make attractive purchases. Considering the number built and the lack of strong identity between years, these will be the affordable Corvettes. New models are getting ever more expensive, and the lower-production older favorites will continue to skyrocket. The 1973-77 series will likely emerge as the "drivers," the Corvettes easiest to buy and sell at modest prices.

1975 Corvette convertible. Author photo.

1973 Corvette Colors/Options

Color Code	Body Color	Soft Top Color
922	Medium Blue	Black/White
927	Dark Blue	Black/White
945	Blue-Green	Black/White
947	Elkhart Green	Black/White
980	Orange	Black/White
976	Mille Miglia Red	Black/White
914	Silver	Black/White
910	Classic White	Black/White
952	Yellow	Black/White
953	Yellow (Metallic)	Black/White

INTERIOR COLORS: Black, Midnight Blue, Dark Red, Dark Saddle, Medium Saddle

Order #	Item Description	Sticker Price
1YZ37	Base Corvette Sport Coupe	5561.50
1YZ67	Base Corvette Convertible	5398.50
—	Custom Interior Trim	154.00
A31	Electric Power Windows	83.00
A85	Custom Shoulder Belts	41.00
C07	Auxiliary Hardtop (for roadster)	267.00
C08	Vinyl Roof Covering for Auxiliary Hardtop	62.00
C50	Rear Window Defroster	41.00
C60	Air Conditioning	452.00
—	Positraction Axle, Optional Ratio	12.00
J50	Power Brakes	46.00
L82	Optional 250 HP, 350 CI Engine	299.00
LS4	Optional 275 HP, 454 CI Engine	250.00
M21	4-Speed Close Ratio Transmission	nc
M40	Turbo Hydramatic Transmission	nc
N37	Tilt-Telescopic Steering Column	82.00
N40	Power Steering	113.00
P02	Custom Wheel Covers	62.00
QRM	White Stripe SBR Tires, GR70x15	32.00
QRZ	White Letter SBR Tires, GR70x15	45.00
T60	Heavy Duty Battery	15.00
U58	AM-FM Stereo Radio	276.00
U69	AM-FM Radio	173.00
UF1	Map Light	5.00
YJ8	Cast Aluminum Wheels	175.00
Z07	Off Road Suspension and Brake Package	369.00

1974 Corvette Colors/Options

Color Code	Body Color	Soft Top Color
922	Corvette Med Blue	Black/White
968	Dark Brown	Black/White
917	Corvette Gray	Black/White
910	Classic White	Black/White
980	Corvette Orange	Black/White
976	Mille Miglia Red	Black/White
974	Medium Red	Black/White
914	Silver Mist	Black/White
948	Dark Green	Black/White
946	Bright Yellow	Black/White

INTERIOR COLORS: Black, Dark Blue, Neutral, Dark Red, Saddle, Silver

Order #	Item Description	Sticker Price
1YZ37	Base Corvette Sport Coupe	6001.50
1YZ67	Base Corvette Convertible	5765.50
—	Custom Interior Trim	154.00
A31	Electric Power Windows	86.00
A85	Custom Shoulder Belts	41.00
C07	Auxiliary Hardtop (for roadster)	267.00
C08	Vinyl Covered Auxiliary Hardtop	329.00
C50	Rear Window Defroster	43.00
C60	Air Conditioning	467.00
FE7	Gymkhana Suspension	7.00
—	Positraction Axle, Optional Ratio	12.00
J50	Power Brakes	49.00
L82	Optional 250 HP, 350 CI Engine	299.00
LS4	Optional 270 HP, 454 CI Engine	250.00
M21	4-Speed Close Ratio Transmission	nc
M40	Turbo Hydramatic Transmission	nc
N37	Tilt-Telescopic Steering Column	82.00
N41	Power Steering	117.00
QRM	White Stripe SBR Tires, GR70x15	32.00
QRZ	White Letter SBR Tires, GR70x15	45.00
U05	Dual Horns	4.00
U58	AM-FM Stereo Radio	276.00
U69	AM-FM Radio	173.00
UA1	Heavy Duty Battery	15.00
UF1	Map Light	5.00
Z07	Off Road Suspension and Brake Package	400.00

1973-1974-1975-1976-1977 Corvette

BASE ENGINE

Type: . . . . Chevrolet ohv V-8

Bore x stroke, inches: . . . . 4.00 x 3.48

Displacement, inches: 350

Compression ratio: 8.5:1

Carburetion: . . . . Single four-barrel carburetor

Horsepower: . . . 190 (1973), 195 (1974), 165 (1975), 180 (1976-7)

Distributor: . . . Single point breaker (1973, 1974), high energy ignition (1975, 1976, 1977)

Other engines offered: . . . Higher horsepower variations were available in 1973, 1974, 1975, 1976 and 1977. See option charts.

CHASSIS AND DRIVETRAIN

Clutch: . . . . Single dry-plate (manual)

Transmission: . . Four-speed manual or three-speed automatic

Front suspension: . . . Coil springs, tube-type shock absorbers, stabilizer bar

Rear suspension: . . . Single transverse leaf spring, tube-type shock absorbers, independent with lateral struts

Axle ratio: . . . . 3.36:1 (manual), 3.08:1 (automatic)

Frame: . . . . Steel box sections, welded

GENERAL:

Wheelbase, inches: 98

Track, front, inches: 58.7

rear, inches: 59.5

Brakes: . . . . Disc, four-wheel

Tire size, front and rear: GR70-15

Wheels: . . . . Steel

Body material: . . . . Fiberglass

Assembly plant: . . . . St. Louis, Missouri

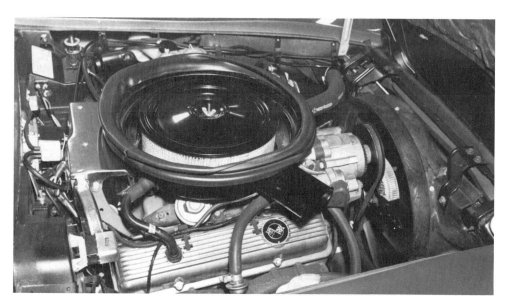

1974 L-82 engine. Author photo.

The 1974 Corvette was the first with the soft body-colored rear. Note that the 1974 at left had a two-piece rear cap section. The 1975 rear cap was redesigned as one piece and had two little fake bumpers molded in at the corners. Author photos.

1975 interior with leather trim. Ed Olson photo.

As was the case in the rear, designers added little bumper pads to the body-colored front end cap of the 1975. They were styled to look like black rubber pads, but were actually molded as part of the cap and painted black. They did have the effect of giving both ends of the 1975 a slimmer, less blunt appearance. Author photos.

 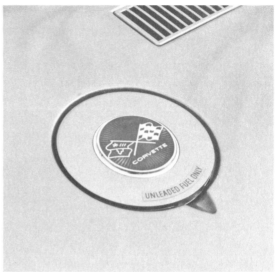

Radios were not standard equipment in Corvettes until 1979 but very few Corvettes left the factory without one. This 1975 is one that did. Some collectors attach special value to no-radio Corvettes because of their scarcity, something most owners who use their cars for pleasure would disagree with. At right, the 1975 was the first Corvette to require unleaded fuel. Ed Olson and author photos.

1976 base engine. Author photo.

This style of aluminum wheel was first available on the 1973 Corvette, but Chevrolet rejected the wheels supplied by a California vendor and attempted to recall those that had been released. The wheel appeared again in 1976 in the same style but produced by Kelsey-Hayes in its Mexican facility (and so identified on the wheel's interior surface). Author photo.

1975 Corvette Colors/Options

Color Code	Body Color	Soft Top Color
22	Bright Blue	Black/White
27	Steel Blue	Black/White
42	Bright Green	Black/White
70	Orange Flame	Black/White
74	Dark Red	Black/White
76	Mille Miglia Red	Black/White
67	Medium Saddle	Black/White
13	Silver	Black/White
10	Classic White	Black/White
56	Bright Yellow	Black/White

INTERIOR COLORS: Black, Dark Blue, Neutral, Dark Red, Medium Saddle, Silver

Order #	Item Description	Sticker Price
1YZ37	Base Corvette Sport Coupe	6810.10
1YZ67	Base Corvette Convertible	6550.10
—	Custom Interior Trim	154.00
A31	Electric Power Windows	93.00
A85	Custom Shoulder Belts	41.00
C07	Auxiliary Hardtop (for roadsters)	267.00
C08	Vinyl Covered Auxiliary Hardtop	350.00
C50	Rear Window Defroster	46.00
C60	Air Conditioning	490.00
FE7	Gymkhana Suspension	7.00
—	Positraction Axle, Optional Ratio	12.00
J50	Power Brakes	50.00
L82	Optional 205 HP, 350 CI Engine	336.00
M21	4-Speed Close Ratio Transmission	nc
M40	Turbo Hydramatic Transmission	nc
N37	Tilt-Telescopic Steering Column	82.00
N41	Power Steering	129.00
QRM	White Stripe SBR Tires. GR70x15	35.00
QRZ	White Letter SBR Tires, GR70x15	48.00
U05	Dual Horns	4.00
U58	AM-FM Stereo Radio	284.00
U69	AM-FM Radio	178.00
UA1	Heavy Duty Battery	15.00
UF1	Map Light	5.00
Z07	Off Road Suspension and Brake Package	400.00

1976 Corvette Colors/Options

Color Code	Body Color
22	Bright Blue
69	Dark Brown
64	Buckskin
33	Dark Green
37	Mahogany
70	Orange Flame
72	Red
13	Silver
10	Classic White
56	Bright Yellow

INTERIOR COLORS: Black, Firethorn, Buckskin, Smoked Grey, Dark Brown, Blue-Green, White

Order #	Item Description	Sticker Price
1YZ37	Base Corvette Sport Coupe	7604.85
—	Custom Interior Trim	164.00
A31	Power Windows	107.00
C49	Rear Window Defogger	78.00
C60	Air Conditioning	523.00
FE7	Gymkhana Suspension	35.00
—	Positraction Axle, Optional Ratio	13.00
J50	Power Brakes	59.00
L82	Optional 210 HP, 350 CI Engine	481.00
M21	4-Speed Close Ratio Transmission	nc
M40	Turbo Hydramatic Transmission	nc
N37	Tilt-Telescopic Steering Column	95.00
N40	Power Steering	151.00
QRM	White Stripe SBR Tires, GR70x15	37.00
QRZ	White Letter SBR Tires, GR70x15	51.00
U58	AM-FM Stereo Radio	281.00
U69	AM-FM Radio	187.00
UA1	Heavy Duty Battery	16.00
UF1	Map Light	10.00
YJ8	Aluminum Wheels	299.00

Enthusiasts didn't care for the addition of the Vega steering wheel to the 1976 interior and it lasted just one year. The 1976 was the last Corvette with the center console style shown, which required a unique radio because of space limitations. Author photo.

The 1977 center console was new and had additional radio room so that the entire range of Delco products would fit. The steering wheel and column were new for 1977 and the headlight dimmer switch, windshield wiper and windshield washer controls all moved to the steering column. Author photos.

1977 Corvette. Chevrolet photo.

Corvettes built in the 1973-77 period weren't known for blistering speed, as engineers struggled to meet ever more stringent federal emission standards. The 1977 L-82 engine shown was rated at 210 hp, a far cry from the 435 hp available a decade earlier. Author photo.

1977 Corvette Colors/Options

Color Code	Body Color
19	Black
28	Corvette Dark Blue
26	Corvette Light Blue
66	Corvette Orange
83	Corvette Dark Red
72	Medium Red
13	Silver
80	Corvette Tan
10	Classic White
52	Corvette Yellow

INTERIOR COLORS: Black, Blue, Brown, Buckskin, Red, Smoked Grey, White

Order #	Item Description	Sticker Price
1YZ37	Base Corvette Sport Coupe	8647.65
A31	Power Windows	116.00
B32	Color Keyed Floor Mats	22.00
C49	Rear Window Defogger	84.00
C60	Air Conditioning	553.00
D35	Sport Mirrors	36.00
FE7	Gymkhana Suspension	38.00
G95	Positraction Axle, Optional Ratio	14.00
K30	Cruise Control	88.00
L82	Optional 210 HP, 350 CI Engine	495.00
M21	4-Speed Close Ratio Transmission	nc
M40	Turbo Hydramatic Transmission	nc
N37	Tilt-Telescopic Steering Column	165.00
QRZ	White Letter SBR Tires, GR70x15	57.00
UA1	Heavy Duty Battery	17.00
U58	AM-FM Stereo Radio	281.00
U69	AM-FM Radio	187.00
UM2	AM-FM Stereo Radio W/Tape System	414.00
V54	Luggage And Roof Panel Rack	73.00
YJ8	Aluminum Wheels	321.00
ZN1	Trailer Package	83.00
ZX2	Convenience Group	22.00

<table>
<tr><td>

CHAPTER 12
1978 CORVETTE

</td><td>

✪✪✪ (Silver Anniversary)
✪✪✪✪ (Pace Car)

</td></tr>
</table>

Serial Nos. 1Z87L8S400001 - 1Z87L8S440274*
            1Z87L8S900001 - 1Z87L8S906502* (Pace Car)
            (*fifth digit varies with engine installed)

It wasn't all-new, but the 1978 was the most changed Corvette since 1968. It was the Corvette's silver anniversary, twenty-five years since the introduction of the Blue Flame six-cylinder. Chevrolet celebrated by adding some nice improvements to the 1978.

For starters, the Corvette became a full fastback again. The restyling of the Corvette's rear doubled the usable area behind the seats, a real shortcoming of the post-1968 cars.

On the inside, Chevrolet finished what was started in 1977. The 1977 got a new console, but in the 1978 the rest of the dash was new. It even got a real glovebox. Inner door panels were redone. The windshield wiper and washer controls moved back to the dash after a one-year stint on the turn-signal lever.

Chevrolet further commemorated the Corvette's twenty-fifth with a two-tone silver paint scheme. These are not special models, just optional paint choices. But some options, like aluminum wheels, had to be purchased when the special paint was ordered. There is no way to differentiate a silver anniversary paint Corvette by its serial numbers.

Not so for the 1978 Corvette Pace Car replica. This is the car that had the world talking about Corvettes again; and it's a great story.

It began when Chevrolet accepted an invitation from the Indianapolis Motor Speedway to provide a pace vehicle for the 1978 race. Early on, it was decided by Chevrolet management that the Corvette would pace the race and that a special model would be created to do it. And replicas would be sold to the public.

What wasn't immediately clear was just what the car would be and how many would be sold. Initially, it was to be two shades of silver with a red dividing stripe, but this changed to silver and black to set it off more from the silver anniversary paint option. There was talk of special Goodyear tires with Corvette spelled out in the sidewalls in white letters. Novel idea, but it was scrubbed due to cost and anticipated replacement headaches.

The first rumored quantity was 300, obviously picked to honor those first 300 Corvettes made in Flint. Next it was 1,000, then 5,000. But long before the Pace Cars were actually built, things were heating up and Chevrolet feared the wrath of its dealers and possible legal action resulting from not providing at least one Pace Car to each. So that's what it did. The final quantity built, 6,502, was based on one for every dealer plus a handful of extras for promotional purposes.

After a few years of hibernation, new Corvettes were being talked about again in 1978. It was the Corvette's twenty-fifth anniversary and Chevrolet celebrated by introducing the most-improved Corvette in a decade, including two specials: the silver anniversary model and the limited edition Pace Car replica. Author photos.

This was no longer a small quantity by any collector's standards, but Pace Car hysteria was already in full bloom and it didn't matter. The cars came into dealerships with a sticker of $13,653.21 which included most options. But the cars soon changed hands for $25,000 and more. Some dealers who had committed themselves to selling their Pace Car at or below sticker price tried to back out. Many got sued as a result.

To put it mildly, the Pace Car Corvette caused a commotion. *The Wall Street Journal* even got into the picture with a front-page article on the mania, quoting some "experts" who predicted prices of $50,000 and more.

Of course it was not to be. Six thousand cars with special paint schemes and a few other geegaws do not a true collector car make. Six thousand is still twenty times the number of 1953's built and few of those would bring $50,000 in 1978. No one is sure what the most paid for a Pace Car was—probably somewhere in the mid-thirties for an L-82 with four-speed transmission, the combination deemed best. The Pace Car basked in the hype until the Indy race, then the bottom fell out. Ads appeared for a long time with exorbitant prices, and still do, but it wasn't too long before Pace Cars were selling for close to their original sticker prices.

All this aside, the 1978 models are among the few in the whole 1968-82 range of Corvettes that come close to being real collector cars. It was a year people recognized and talked about. It was a well-built car and most people viewed the new rear window treatment, interior redesign and a larger fuel tank as definite improvements.

What isn't so clear is which 1978 models will prove to be the best investments in the long run. While the Pace Car is thought to be too gaudy for many tastes, the silver anniversary paint scheme is widely popular. All Pace Car replica Corvettes had silver cloth or leather interiors. Even more silver anniversary paint 1978's were built, but these could be ordered with any interior color. Perhaps a rare silver anniversary paint trim combination, such as dark blue leather, will emerge from the herd.

Maybe it'll still be the Pace Car. It was one of the most publicized Corvettes ever. Publicity alone doesn't create classic cars and there are still too many new Pace Cars tucked away in garages for any great price explosion to occur. But over the years, as other Corvettes of the era fade away, the Pace Car may yet emerge as the high-dollar Corvette of the period. It does have unique credentials.

1978 Corvette

BASE ENGINE

Type: . . . . Chevrolet ohv V-8
Bore x stroke, inches: . . . . 4.00 x 3.48
Displacement, inches: 350
Compression ratio: 8.2:1
Carburetion: . . . . Single four-barrel carburetor
Horsepower: 185
Distributor: . . . . High energy ignition
Other engines offered:. . .A 220-hp engine was optional in 1978

CHASSIS AND DRIVETRAIN

Clutch: . . . . Single dry-plate (manual)
Transmission:. . .Four-speed manual or three-speed automatic

Front suspension:. . .Coil springs, tube-type shock absorbers, stabilizer bar
Rear suspension:. . .Single transverse leaf spring, tube-type shock absorbers, independent with lateral struts
Axle ratio: . . . . .3.36:1 (manual), 3.08:1 (automatic)
Frame: . . . . Steel box sections, welded

GENERAL:

Wheelbase, inches: 98
Track, front, inches: 58.7
rear, inches: 59.5
Brakes: . . . . Disc, four-wheel
Tire size, front and rear: P255/70 R-15
Wheels: . . . . .Steel
Body material: . . . . .Fiberglass
Assembly plant: . . . . .St. Louis, Missouri

The limited edition Pace Car Corvette came with a silver interior in either leather or cloth trimmed in leather. The seats were a completely new design unique to the Pace Car in 1978, but standard in all Corvettes starting in 1979. The main instrument cluster was new for 1978 in all Corvettes and was beautifully executed. Ed Olson Photos.

The center console designed for the new 1978 interior actually appeared in 1977. But the 1978 was the first to have an AM-FM radio with CB available . . . at a whopping $638. Ed Olson and author photos.

The limited edition Pace Car replica Corvette is perhaps the most famous Corvette in recent memory. These were being sold for double their sticker price even before their release. Many dealers renigged on purchase agreements in attempts to squeeze more profits; and the subsequent law suits, bad publicity and ill will left a cloud over what was one of the finer Corvettes in modern history. The inflated price bubble burst shortly after the Indy 500 race in 1978 and Pace Car replicas can now be purchased for very reasonable prices. Author photo.

The lesser-known special Corvette in 1978 was the silver anniversary edition. This was just a paint option, but the two-tone silver Corvette offered an excellent alternative to those who felt the Pace Car Corvette was too gaudy. Defying logic, the silver anniversary 1978 Corvettes have held their value nearly as well as the Pace Cars. Author photo.

"CORVETTE PACES INDY 500 — A special 'Limited Edition' Corvette will lead the 33-car field at the 62nd annual Indianapolis 500 race May 28, 1978. The pace car features two-tone black and silver paint treatment along with front air dam, rear deck lid spoiler, polished aluminum spoked wheels with red stripe, glass roof panels, white-lettered tires, sport mirrors, special 'smoke' color interior and 'Indy Pace Car' decals on the front fenders. The L-82 high performance 350-cubic inch (5.7 liter) V-8 with Turbo Hydramatic transmission will power the vehicle. This year also marks Corvette's 25th anniversary in the Chevrolet lineup as America's one-of-a-kind sports car." Chevrolet press release from 1978. Chevrolet photos.

1978 Corvette Colors/Options

Color Code	Body Color
59	Corvette Light Beige
19	Black
83	Corvette Dark Blue
26	Corvette Light Blue
89	Corvette Dark Brown
82	Corvette Mahogany
72	Corvette Red
13	Silver
13	Silver Anniversary
10	Classic White
52	Corvette Yellow

INTERIOR COLORS: Black, Dark Blue, Light Beige, Red, Mahogany, Oyster

Order #	Item Description	Sticker Price
1YZ87	Corvette Sport Coupe	9351.89
1YZ87/78	Limited Edition Corvette (Pace Car)	13,653.21
A31	Power Windows	130.00
AU3	Power Door Locks	120.00
B2Z	Silver Anniversary Paint	399.00
CC1	Removable Glass Roof Panels	349.00
C49	Rear Window Defogger	95.00
C60	Air Conditioning	605.00
D35	Sport Mirrors	40.00
FE7	Gymkhana Suspension	41.00
G95	Positraction Axle, Optional Highway Ratio	15.00
K30	Cruise Control	99.00
L82	Optional 220 HP, 350 CI Engine	525.00
M21	4-Speed Close Ratio Transmission	nc
MX1	Turbo Hydramatic Transmission	nc
N37	Tilt-Telescopic Steering Column	175.00
QBS	White Letter SBR Tires, P255/60 R-15	216.32
QGR	White Letter SBR Tires, P255/70 R-15	51.00
UA1	Heavy Duty Battery	18.00
UM2	AM-FM Stereo Radio W/Tape System	419.00
UP6	AM-FM Stereo Radio W/CB System	638.00
U58	AM-FM Stereo Radio	286.00
U69	AM-FM Radio	199.00
U75	Power Antenna	49.00
U81	Dual Rear Speakers	49.00
YJ8	Aluminum Wheels	340.00
ZN1	Trailer Package	89.00
ZX2	Convenience Group	84.00

Chevrolet used the aluminum wheels available since 1976 for the Pace Car Corvette but polished them to a bright finish and added a red tape stripe. Limited edition stickers appeared on the Pace Car but the big Indy 500 decals for the doors and rear fenders were packed loose with the car for installation by the owner. Most chose not to use them. Author photos.

CHAPTER 13

Serial Nos. 1979: 1Z8789S400001 - 1Z8789S453807
1980: 1Z878AS400001 - 1Z878AS440614
1981: 1G1AY8764BS400001 - 1G1AY8764BS431611
(St. Louis)
1981: 1G1AY8764B5400001 - 1G1AY8764B5108995
(Bowling Green)
1982: 1G1AY8786C5100001 -1G1AY8786C5125407
(sixth digit for 1982 Collector Edition is a 0)
(ninth digit for 1981-82 is a check digit and
varies)

Rumors of a "brand-new Corvette next year" have been part of the Corvette scene since its earliest days. Finally, the rumors heard around 1979 were based on fact. A new Corvette really was on the way for 1983.

The Corvette chassis introduced in 1963 models had a twenty-year life and the 1968 body style lasted fifteen. Considering the upheaval the industry went through during these years, the longevity of the Corvette body and chassis designs is a tribute to the soundness of both. All in all, this is one of auto history's more successful series of cars.

But it came to an end. The 1979-82 models were the end of the series. They were thought of as those built after the anniversary/Pace Car year and before the new generation. With a new car coming, major changes weren't in the cards for the 1979-82 models, but notable things did happen.

The 1979 Corvette carried the same body as the 1978 except for detail changes like emblems. The new-style seat introduced in the Pace Car became standard equipment in 1979. These seats employed extensive plastic to cut weight. Also, the front and rear bolt-on spoilers, which made their debut on the Pace Car, became optional on the 1979. Chevrolet reported these capable of reducing aerodynamic drag by fifteen percent. Nineteen seventy-nine production reached 53,807.

In 1980, new bumper caps for both the front and rear were introduced. These had integral spoilers which eliminated the add-on appearance of the previous type. They offered aerodynamic gains and a fifty-percent increase of airflow into the radiator.

Engineers went after weight reductions in the 1980 model. An aluminum differential housing and cross-member replaced steel units. Fiberglass body panels, door and windshield glass, and the frame were all made thinner. A 350-cubic-inch engine was standard in all states except California which got a 305-cubic-incher. To the horror of Corvette enthusiasts, a federal mandate resulted in a speedometer with a maximum reading of 85 mph. Production for the year totaled 40,614.

1980 Corvette. Chevrolet photo.

Some of the 1978 Pace Car Corvette features rubbed off onto the 1979 production Corvettes. The bolt-on front air dam and rear spoiler became options for the 1979. But the silver anniversary emblems that adorned the 1978 were removed and the 1979 emblems were the same as those used in 1977. Author photos.

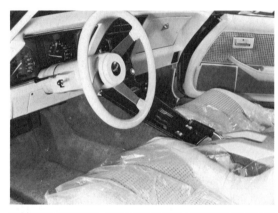

The Pace Car influence was also evident in the interior of the 1979. The new seat design used first in the Pace Car became the standard seat for 1979. This unusual checkered fabric was also tried in 1979. Author photos.

1979 Corvette Colors/Options

Color Code	Body Color
59	Corvette Light Beige
19	Black
83	Corvette Dark Blue
28	Corvette Light Blue
82	Corvette Dark Brown
58	Corvette Dark Green
72	Corvette Red
13	Silver
52	Corvette Yellow
10	Classic White

INTERIOR COLORS: Black, Dark Blue, Dark Brown, Light Beige, Red, Dark Green, Oyster

Order #	Item Description	Sticker Price
1YZ87	Corvette Sport Coupe	10,220.23
A31	Power Windows	141.00
CC1	Removable Glass Roof Panels	365.00
C49	Rear Window Defogger	102.00
C60	Air Conditioning	635.00
D35	Sport Mirrors	45.00
FE7	Gymkhana Suspension	49.00
F51	Heavy Duty Shock Absorbers	33.00
G95	Highway Ratio Rear Axle	19.00
K30	Cruise Control	113.00
L82	Optional 225 HP, 350 CI Engine	565.00
MM4	4-Speed Transmission	nc
M21	4-Speed Transmission, Close Ratio	nc
MX1	Turbo-Hydramatic Transmission	nc
N37	Tilt-telescopic Steering Column	190.00
N90	Aluminum Wheels	380.00
QGR	White Letter SBR Tires, P225/70 R-15	54.00
QBS	White Letter Aramid BR Tires, P225/60 R-15	226.20
U58	AM/FM Stereo Radio	90.00
UM2	AM/FM Stereo Radio w/tape	228.00
UN3	AM/FM Stereo Radio w/cassette	234.00
UP6	AM/FM Stereo Radio w/CB and power antenna	439.00
U75	Power Antenna	52.00
U81	Dual Rear Speakers	52.00
UA1	Heavy Duty Battery	21.00
ZN1	Trailer Package	98.00
ZQ2	Power Windows and Door Locks	272.00
ZX2	Convenience Group	94.00

1980 Corvette Colors/Options

Color Code	Body Color
19	Black
13	Silver
58	Dark Green
83	Red
52	Yellow
28	Dark Blue
59	Frost Beige
76	Dark Claret
47	Dark Brown
10	White

INTERIOR COLORS: Black, Oyster, Red, Dark Blue, Claret, Doeskin

Order #	Item Description	Sticker Price
1YZ87	Corvette Sport Coupe	13,140.24
AU3	Power Door Locks	140.00
CC1	Removable Glass Roof Panels	391.00
C49	Rear Window Defogger	109.00
FE7	Gymkhana Suspension	55.00
F51	Heavy Duty Shock Absorbers	35.00
K30	Cruise Control	123.00
LG4	180 HP, 305 CI Engine (Req'd California)	−50.00
L48	190 HP, 350 CI Engine (Base except Calif)	nc
L82	230 HP, 350 CI Engine	595.00
MM4	4-Speed Transmission	nc
MX1	4-Speed Transmission, Close Ratio	nc
MX1	Trubo-Hydramatic Transmission	nc
N90	Aluminum Wheels	407.00
QGB	White Letter SBR Tires, P225/70 R-15	62.00
QXH	White Letter SBR Tires, P225/60 R-15	426.16
UA1	Heavy Duty Battery	22.00
U58	AM/FM Stereo Radio	46.00
UM2	AM/FM Stereo Radio w/8-track	155.00
UN3	AM/FM Stereo Radio w/cassette	168.00
UP6	AM/FM Stereo Radio w/CB and power antenna	391.00
U75	Power Antenna	56.00
UL5	Radio Delete	−126.00
U81	Dual Rear Speakers	52.00
V54	Roof Panel Carrier	125.00
YF5	California Emissions	250.00
ZN1	Trailer Package	105.00

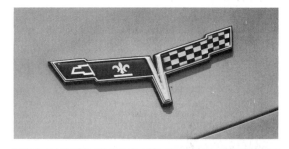

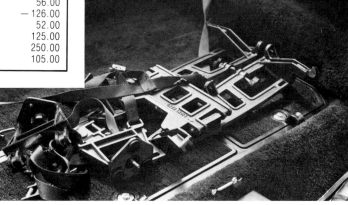

Detail changes for 1980 included a new side fender treatment, new emblems and a new apparatus to attach the roof panels to the rear deck area of the exterior. Author photos.

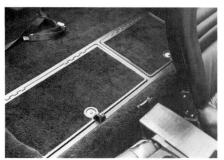

Aerodynamics became the key word in auto design for the eighties, and Corvette designers improved airflow over the Corvette by incorporating a front air dam and rear spoiler into the bumper caps. The storage bins behind the seats were reduced from three to two in 1980 and the hand of the government struck again in the form of a speedometer in America's premier sports car that could read to only 85 mph. Author photos.

The Corvette changed little in 1981. Chevrolet photo.

1981 Corvette Colors/Options

Color Code	Body Color
75	Red
52	Yellow
19	Black
10	White
59	Beige
13	Silver Metallic
28	Dark Blue Metallic
24	Bright Blue Metallic
79	Maroon Metallic
84	Charcoal Metallic
33/38M	Silver/Dark Blue
50/74M	Beige/Dark Bronze
33/39M	Silver/Charcoal
80/98M	Claret/Dark Claret

INTERIOR COLORS: Camel, Blue, Black, Rust, Red, Silver

Order #	Item Description	Sticker Price
1YY87	Corvette Coupe	16,258.52
L81	5.7 Liter V-8 engine	nc
G92	Performance Rear Axle	20.00
V54	Roof Panel Carrier	135.00
ZN1	Trailering Equipment	110.00
C49	Rear Window Defogger	119.00
AU3	Power Door Locks	145.00
DG7	Electric Sport Mirrors	117.00
U58	AM/FM Stereo Radio	95.00
UM4	Electronically Tuned Stereo/8-track	386.00
UM5	Electronically Tuned Stereo/CB/ 8-track	712.00
UN5	Electronically Tuned Stereo/CB/ Cassette	750.00
UM6	Electronically Tuned Stereo/Cassette	423.00
U75	Power Antenna	55.00
UL5	Radio Delete	−118.00
CC1	Removable Glass Roof Panels	414.00
A42	Power Driver's Seat	183.00
F51	Heavy Duty Shock Absorbers	37.00
K35	Cruise Control w/Resume	155.00
FE7	Gymkhana Suspension	57.00
QGR	White Letter SBR Tires, P225/60R-15	72.00
QXH	White Letter SBR Tires, P255/60R-15	491.92
MM4	4-Speed Transmission	nc
MX1	Turbo-Hydramatic Transmission	nc
N90	Aluminum Wheels	428.00
D84	Two-Tone Exterior Paint	399.00

1982 Corvette Colors/Options

Color Code	Body Color
19	Black
31	Bright Blue
26	Dark Blue
24	Silver Blue
39	Charcoal
99	Dark Claret
56	Gold
40	Silver Green
70	Red
13	Silver
10	White
59	Silver Beige (Collector)
24/26M	Silver Blue/Dark Blue
13/99M	Silver/Dark Claret
13/39M	Silver/Charcoal
10/13M	White/Silver

INTERIOR COLORS: Dark Blue, Camel, Charcoal, Dark Red, Silver Grey, Silver Green, Silver Beige

Order #	Item Description	Sticker Price
1YY87	Corvette Coupe	18,290.07
1YY07	Collector Edition Hatchback	22,537.59
D84	Two-Tone Exterior Paint	428.00
L83	5.7 Liter V-8 Engine	nc
V54	Roof Panel Carrier	144.00
V08	Heavy Duty Cooling	57.00
C49	Rear Window Defogger	129.00
AU3	Power Door Locks	155.00
DG7	Electric Sport Mirrors	125.00
U58	AM/FM Stereo Radio	101.00
UM4	Electronically Tuned Stereo/8-track	386.00
UN5	Electronically Tuned Stereo/ CB/Cassette	755.00
	w/1YY07	695.00
UM6	Electronically Tuned Stereo w/Cassette	423.00
U75	Power Antenna	60.00
UL5	Radio Delete	−124.00
CC1	Removable Glass Roof Panels	443.00
AG9	Power Driver's Seat	197.00
K35	Cruise Control w/Resume	165.00
FE7	Gymkhana Suspension	61.00
QGR	White Letter SBR Tires, P225/70R-15	80.00
QXH	White Letter SBR Tires, P255/60R-15	542.52
N90	Aluminum Wheels	458.00

The 1982 collector edition had a tasteful gold and silver paint scheme and very nice detailing. In addition to trim changes, the collector edition differed from other 1982 models by the lifting rear hatch window. But it didn't come cheap. The 1982 collector edition's base price cracked the twenty-thousand-dollar figure for the first time in the Corvette's history at an attention-getting $22,537.59. John Amgwert photos.

1979-1980-1981-1982 Corvette

BASE ENGINE

Type: . . . . .Chevrolet ohv V-8
Bore x stroke, inches: . . . . .4.00 x 3.48*
Displacement, inches: 350*
Compression ratio: . . .8.2:1 (1979, 1980, 1981), 9:1 (1982)
Carburetion:...Single four-barrel carburetor (1979, 1980, 1981), throttle body injection (1982)
Horsepower: 195 (1979), 190 (1980, 1981), 200 (1982)
Distributor: . . . . .High energy ignition
Other engines offered:...*The 350 engine was not certified for sale in California during the 1980 model year. California Corvettes were equipped with 305 engines. See option tables for additional engines available in 1979 and 1980.

CHASSIS AND DRIVETRAIN

Clutch: . . . . .Single dry-plate (manual)
Transmission:...Four-speed manual (1979, 1980, 1981) or three-speed automatic
Front suspension:...Coil springs, tube-type shock absorbers, stabilizer bar
Rear suspension:...Single transverse leaf spring, tube-type shock absorbers, independent with lateral struts
Axle Ratio:...3.36:1 (1979 manual), 3.55:1 (1979 automatic), 3.07:1 (1980), 2.72:1 (1981 manual, 1982), 2.87:1 (1981 automatic, 1982 collectors)
Frame: .Steel box sections, welded

GENERAL:

Wheelbase, inches: 98
Track, front, inches: 58.7
rear, inches: 59.5
Brakes: . . . . .Disc, four-wheel
Tire size, front and rear: P255/70 R-15
Wheels: . . . . .Steel
Body material: . . . . .Fiberglass
Assembly plant:...St. Louis, Missouri (1979, 1980, 1981 partial), Bowling Green, Kentucky (1981 partial, 1982)

The weight-reduction campaign continued in the 1981 models equipped with automatic transmissions and standard suspensions by the replacement of the steel rear leaf spring by a unit made of fiberglass. The steel spring weighed thirty-three pounds, compared to just seven for the plastic spring. Emblems changed slightly, seat design was modified, Californians got the 350-cubic-inch engine again and Delco offered a snazzy new radio.

But the big news for 1981 was the end of Corvette production in St. Louis and the start of production in Bowling Green, Kentucky. St. Louis built its last Corvette on July 31, 1981. Bowling Green built its first on June 1, 1981, so there was a two-month overlap. Production of 1981 models by the St. Louis plant totaled 31,611 compared to 8,995 at Bowling Green.

Even before 1982 production began, enthusiasts drew an analogy between the 1982 and the 1967 and 1962 models, as each ended Corvette eras. Chevrolet thought about this too and created a "Collector Edition" for 1982. Production was not limited and the Collector Edition comprised about thirty percent of 1982 production. It was a beautiful package, featuring silver-gold metallic paint with a clear lacquer overcoat for gloss. It was highly optioned and even had special wheels with a design lifted right from the "bolt-on" cast aluminum wheel of 1967, a particularly interesting touch which confirmed the 1967 analogy.

Other than the Collector Edition, the 1982 body was no different from 1981 models except for small details. But there was news in the engine department. Chevrolet introduced "cross fire injection," also called "throttle body injection." This new fuel-injection system eliminated conventional carburetors and had its function controlled constantly by a small computer. Just as it had done in the 1962-63 transformation years, Chevrolet had chosen to introduce the drive train package ahead of the new body/chassis by one year.

The 1979-82 Corvettes are fine automobiles but will never be collector cars because of the sheer quantity built, their general sameness, and the lack of genuine performance packages. In 1982, for instance, a manual transmission wasn't even available. But even though their body design dates to 1968 and their chassis to 1963, these are refined and very popular automobiles. Tremendous gains in tire design combined with the proven chassis to make these Corvettes handle very well. The space gains of the new rear end design make them much more practical to own. The Collector Edition was the only one with an opening rear window and the stylists' good taste exemplified in the car's trim make it a particularly good choice.

1982 Corvette. Chevrolet photo.

Serial Nos. 1984: 1G1AY0781E5100001 - 1G1AY0781E5151547
1985: 1G1YY0787F5100001 - 1G1YY0787F5139727
1986: 1G1YY0789G5100001 - 1G1YY0789G5127794
(Coupe)
1986: 1G1YY6789G9100001 - 1G1YY6789G9107315
(Convertible)
1987: 1G1YY2182H5100001 - 1G1YY2182H5130632
(sixth digit for 1987 convertibles is a 3)
(ninth digit for all years is a check digit and varies)

"Is this the new Corvette?"

Not a year passed between 1968 and 1982 without at least one of the major auto magazines having that question on its cover, along with a spy photo or artist's sketch. Corvette features do sell magazines, but the editors weren't necessarily being deceptive. Chevrolet *did* start and stop several development programs for the elusive, all-new Corvette.

Each abort is a story in itself, but it can generally be said the Corvette suffered a priority penalty. Building and selling automobiles was a different ball game in the seventies, and General Motors had more important matters to concern itself with than creating a successor for its relatively low-volume sports car.

Zora Arkus-Duntov, the famous Corvette engineering guru, retired in 1975. If one of the Corvette programs started prior to 1975 had seen completion, the new Corvettes today would be mid-engine designs. Duntov, first and foremost an engine genius, saw the logical evolution of the Corvette leading it to mid-engine placement, because the rearward weight bias would put more of the engine's tractive power at the driving wheels.

Duntov's successor was David McLellan, brilliant engineer, veteran of fifteen chassis development years at GM's Milford proving grounds, and a graduate of GM's Sloan Fellowship Management Program. McLellan brought an open mind to the question of a new Corvette's configuration. After thorough analysis, he concluded mid-engine placement created more problems than it solved. While acknowledging the Corvette had grown obsolete, he felt its big front-mounted V-8 driving the rear wheels was still the best configuration to meet the Corvette's mission.

McLellan's vision for an all-new Corvette was at the same time conservative and radical. The engine and its placement would be traditional Corvette, but virtually everything else would be scrapped and replaced with the latest in state-of-the-art thinking. In 1978, McLellan's group began engineering work on the project that resulted in the 1984 Corvette.

Oddly, there was no 1983 Corvette model. What should have been a 1983 Corvette introduction in September 1982 was delayed until March 1983, a simple case of schedule slippage. In the interim, Chevrolet realized its "1983" model

1985 Corvette. Author photos.

could meet 1984 federal regulations and substantial savings achieved by just calling it a 1984 and forgetting about a model changeover six months later. This was much to the dismay of Corvette enthusiasts, especially those proud owners of the Corvette's first year, 1953, who'd written Chevrolet in hopes of getting a 1983 with a corresponding serial number.

The 1984 Corvette catapulted America's sports car into the ranks of the world's best contemporary performance automobiles. In fact, the cornering capability of the new Corvette was nearly beyond belief. You can almost imagine Chevy engineers, after reading endless magazine road tests during the seventies when g-meters and skidpad tests became the rage, saying, "Okay, you want a car that stays glued to the skidpad, we'll give you one." Did they ever! But the cornering asset turned into a liability when the public perceived the car's suspension as bone crushing, and resale values plummeted. Understanding this issue is one key to making a smart purchase of a 1984-87 Corvette. Here's the story:

One indication of cornering ability is how much force it takes to break the tires' adhesion. Magazine testers measure this with a g-meter (a "g" equals the force of gravity) on a skidpad. Where the family sedan might register a 0.70g or less, performance-oriented cars would be in the 0.75g to 0.85g range. Different skidpads yield slightly different results, but readings over 0.85g are always considered exceptional.

Corvette engineers worked with Goodyear to develop a tire-and-suspension combination that would yield very high skidpad adhesion results. Since high cornering adhesion requires minimal body lean, Corvette engineers specified very stiff springs, then combined these springs with other performance items in an option labeled RPO Z51.

Using non-stock camber settings and the RPO Z51, a prototype 1984 Corvette reached 1.01g in GM skidpad tests. Even in showroom trim, GM's tests yielded 0.95g for the Z51 and 0.90g for the base suspension. (*Road & Track*'s September 1986 issue road test summary put the Z51 Corvette at 0.91g, best of seventy five cars tested.) Even before the 1984 Corvette was officially introduced, news of its extraordinary cornering ability was out. The Z51 option had a magic ring; customers demanded it, dealers ordered it, and almost half of the 1984 Corvettes sold were Z51-equipped.

This was ridiculous. The Z51 spring rates were much too hard for everyday driving. After the hoopla surrounding the introduction died down, owners started complaining about the Corvette's harsh ride. The car magazines, universally euphoric at first exposure to the new Corvette (at a smooth Riverside racetrack in California, by the way), changed their tune after extensive road testing. They became critical of the Corvette's ride quality, *Car & Driver* calling it an "F16" kind of car, unsuitable for "civilians." Rough ride wasn't the only problem brought on by the hard suspension; the 1984 was notorious for squeaks and rattles.

Chevrolet reacted quickly. The springs for both Z51 and base suspension 1985 models were softened, so that the Z51 in 1985 rode much like the base suspension of 1984. In 1986, the base suspension was softened again. In 1987, RPO Z52 combined softer base suspension springs with performance items previously part of the Z51 package; things like wider wheels, heavy-duty cooling, and quicker steering. To keep hard suspension models out of unsuspecting hands, Chevrolet started making four-speed manual transmissions mandatory with the Z51 option starting in late 1986. Even as spring rates were reduced, the Corvette's handling

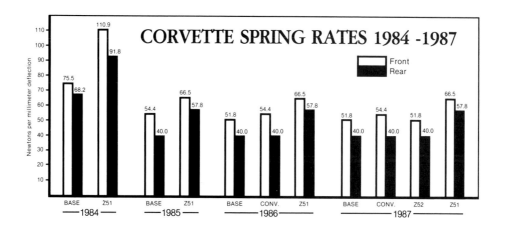

CORVETTE SPRING RATES 1984 -1987

Newtons per millimeter deflection

Legend: Front / Rear

	1984	1985	1986	1987
BASE Front	75.5	54.4	51.8	51.8
BASE Rear	68.2	40.0	40.0	40.0
Z51 Front	110.9	66.5		66.5
Z51 Rear	91.8	57.8		57.8
CONV Front			54.4	54.4
CONV Rear			40.0	40.0
Z51 (1986) Front			66.5	
Z51 (1986) Rear			57.8	
Z52 Front				51.8
Z52 Rear				40.0

1984 Corvette Colors/Options	
Color Code	**Body Color**
10	White
16	Bright Silver
18	Medium Gray
19	Black
20	Light Blue
23	Medium Blue
53	Gold
63	Light Bronze
66	Dark Bronze
72	Bright Red
16/18M	Silver/Gray
20/23M	Light Blue/Medium Blue
63/66M	Light Bronze/Dark Bronze

INTERIOR COLORS: Graphite, Medium Gray, Medium Blue, Light Saddle, Carmine, Dark Bronze

Order #	Item Description	Sticker Price
1YY07	Corvette Sport Coupe	21,800.00
—	Leather Seats	400.00
AG9	Power Driver Seat	210.00
AQ9	Sport Seats (Cloth)	625.00
AU3	Power Door Locks	165.00
CC3	Removable Transparent Roof Panel	595.00
D84	Two-Tone Paint	428.00
FG3	Delco/Bilstein Shock Absorbers	189.00
G92	Performance Axle Ratio	22.00
KC4	Engine Oil Cooler	158.00
K34	Cruise Control	185.00
MM4	4-Speed Transmission	n/c
MX0	Automatic Transmission	n/c
UL5	Radio Delete	-256.00
UM6	Electronically Tuned Stereo/Cassette	153.00
UN8	Electronically Tuned Stereo/CB	215.00
UU8	Delco-Bose Stereo System	895.00
V01	Heavy Duty Radiator	57.00
YF5	California Emissions	75.00
Z51	Performance Handling Package	600.20
Z6A	Defogger System	160.00

1985 Corvette Colors/Options	
Color Code	**Body Color**
13	Silver
18	Medium Gray
20	Light Blue
23	Medium Blue
40	White
41	Black
53	Gold
63	Light Bronze
66	Dark Bronze
81	Bright Red
13/18M	Silver/Gray
20/23M	Light Blue/Medium Blue
63/66M	Light Bronze/Dark Bronze

INTERIOR COLORS: Graphite, Medium Gray, Medium Blue, Light Saddle, Carmine, Dark Bronze

Order #	Item Description	Sticker Price
1YY07	Corvette Sport Coupe	24,878.00
A—2	Leather Seats	400.00
A—8	Sport Seats, Leather	1,025.00
B—8	Sport Seats, Cloth	625.00
AG9	Power Driver Seat	215.00
AU3	Power Door Locks	170.00
CC3	Removable Transparent Roof Panel	595.00
D84	Two-Tone Paint	428.00
FG3	Delco/Bilstein Shock Absorbers	189.00
G92	Performance Axle Ratio	22.00
K34	Cruise Control	185.00
MM4	Four-Speed Transmission	n/c
MM0	Automatic Transmission	n/c
NN5	California Emissions	99.00
UL5	Radio Delete	-256.00
UM6	Electronically Tuned Stereo/Cassette	122.00
UN8	Electronically Tuned Stereo/CB	215.00
UU8	Delco-Bose Stereo System	895.00
V08	Heavy Duty Cooling	225.00
Z51	Performance Handling Package	470.00
Z6A	Defogger System	160.00

improved overall (skidpad numbers did drop a bit) as engineers were able to tweak and tune other chassis components.

Chevrolet specialists scrutinized every assembly process to eliminate potential squeaks or rattles. Overall construciton, including paint quality, improved steadily through 1984 and 1985 and stayed there. By the end of 1986, the Corvette was consistently vying with the Nova (the product of Chevy's joint venture with Toyota) for top spot in Chevrolet's internal quality audits. Engineers were concerned enough about the negative perception of the 1984 Corvette that they made sure magazine writers got 1985 test vehicles well in advance of normal previews. The motoring press reacted favorably, admitting the improvements left little to fault in the Corvette.

Meanwhile, enthusiasts reacted positively to the new Corvette with only a few exceptions. There was criticism of its appearance similarity to the Camaro. There's little argument that the Corvette's exterior was a magnificent design (as was the Camaro's), but the looks comparison was valid, no doubt because both vehicles were designed in the same studio, Chevrolet #3, managed by Jerry Palmer.

The interior's instrumentation also got a mixed reception. The latest in electronics was certainly dazzling, but the graphic speedometer and tach displays were difficult to read quickly. Cost was yet another common complaint, enthusiasts feeling Chevrolet had priced the Corvette beyond reach of too many of its traditional customers.

Here's the bright side. The public's perception of 1984 Corvettes and the number built (51,547) combined to drive resale prices down, and subsequent models got caught in the downslide, though less drastically. Considering the performance capabilities of these automobiles, some used 1984-87 Corvettes are outstanding values. But not all.

To select one of these Corvettes, first ignore the investment angle. Some will eventually appreciate, but selection should be based on personal driving enjoy-

---

1984-1985-1986-1987 Corvette

BASE ENGINE

Type: . . . . .Chevrolet ohv V-8
Bore x stroke, inches: .4.00 x 3.48
Displacement, inches: 350
Compression ratio: .9.0:1 (1984), 9.5:1 (1985, 1986, 1987)
Carburetion: . . . . . . throttle body injection (1984), tuned-port injection 1985, 1986, 1987)
Horsepower: 205 (1984), 230 (1985, 1986), 240 (1987)
Distributor: . . . . .High energy ignition
Other engines offered: . . . . .Base engines were the only ones available in 1984, 1985 and 1986. In 1987, a Callaway Twin Turbo engine was available through Chevrolet dealers. The engine was built and installed by Callaway Engineering, but had standard emissions and the full Corvette warranty.

CHASSIS AND DRIVETRAIN

Clutch: . . . . .Single dry-plate (manual)
Transmissions:. . 4-speed automatic with overdrive and high stall torque converter; 4-speed manual with computer-controlled overdrive (manual override) in 2nd, 3rd, and 4th gears.

Front suspension: . . . . . .Single transverse leaf spring, tube-type shock absorbers, upper and lower A-arms, stabilizer bar.

Rear suspension: . . .Single transverse leaf spring, tube-type shock absorbers, upper and lower control arms, stabilizer bar.

Frame: . . . . . . .All-welded body-frame integral construction. Bolt-in front crossmember to allow bottom-loaded engine.

General:

Wheelbase, inches:. 96.2
Track, front, inches:. 59.6
     rear, inches: 60.4
Brakes:. . . . . .Disc, four-wheel
Tire size, front and rear:. P255/50VR-16
Wheel material:. . . . . .Aluminum alloy
Wheel sizes, inches: . . . . .16 x 8.5, 16 x 9.5
Body material: . . . . .Fiberglass
Assembly plant: . . . . .Bowling Green, Kentucky

No one could deny the 1984 Corvette was one beautiful automobile. Its engine, shown at left, had a magnesium cover over its cross-fire injection fuel delivery system. For 1985-87 models, tuned-port injection (right) replaced the cross-fire, yielding both power and economy gains. Author photos.

For 1986-87 Corvette coupes, the mandatory central-mount stoplamp was located on top of the hatch hinge; for convertibles, it was in the rear facia above the Corvette name script. Author photos.

In 1986, for the first time in more than a decade, Corvette enthusiasts had a choice of either coupe or convertible models. The new convertible was built by Chevrolet in its Corvette facility in Bowling Green, Kentucky, but still cost $5,005 more than the coupe. Both models featured anti-lock brakes. The convertibles and later-production coupes also had aluminum cylinder heads. Chevrolet photo.

Leather sport seats (above left), had controls in the bolsters and were available in 1985-87 models. The standard seat was cloth (above right); the 1986-87 base cloth is shown. Chevrolet made small improvements to the instruments, including tilting the displays as shown in these 1986 model photos, but stayed with the electronic displays through the 1984-87 period. Author photos.

ment criteria. As others learn to do the same, yours will be that much more valuable.

Unlike earlier Corvettes which are sold primarily between individuals and specialty dealers, used 1984-87 Corvettes are mixed in with everything else in the used-car market. This means that a good percentage of the selling dealers aren't any more knowledgeable about Corvettes than the scores of other models they deal with. With Corvettes, they know reds and blacks are strong sellers, blues aren't, and other colors are somewhere between. They think automatics are easier to sell than four-speeds, and leather interiors are easier than cloth. Beyond that, they figure the more options, the better. These aren't bad criteria, just incomplete.

Color might be a resale consideration for a buyer who doesn't plan to keep a new Corvette long. Beyond that, it's not so clear. The popular colors are the safest choices, but the scarcity of some of the low runners can be an advantage in the long run. After all, some of the less common colors, like 1984-85's Dark Bronze and 1986-87's Silver Beige, are quite beautiful. Then again, a lousy color is a lousy color, scarce or not.

Like the popular colors, automatic-transmission Corvettes are the safer choices. Chevrolet sold about four automatic Corvettes to each four-speed in the 1984-87 period. But if hardcore enthusiasts are drawn to used 1984-87 Corvettes for their performance value, and if hardcores prefer manual shifting, four-speeds could be in short supply.

Leather seating has been preferred to cloth in the 1984-87 Corvettes by about the same eighty-percent margin as automatics to four-speeds. There were three seat choices with 1984 models, a base seat in a muted cloth, a base seat in optional leather, and an optional "sport" seat in a not-so-muted checkerboard cloth. Midway in 1985 production, leather became available in the sport seat, so for half of that model year there were four choices. For 1986 and 1987, the sport seat was available only in leather, and the base seat in cloth or optional leather as before, except that the cloth was the style previously used for the sport seats. Got that?

The earlier cloth was the better looking of the two. The most comfortable combination was the cloth sport seat of 1984 and 1985. Leather seats had a certain mystique and sold best because they looked better when new than the cloth choices, but they didn't wear as well as either cloth.

Chevrolet was selected for the Indy 500 pace car privilege in 1986 and used the occasion to showcase the return of a Corvette convertible, the first since 1975. Designed by Chevrolet with assistance from the American Sunroof Company, also factory-built by Chevrolet, the ragtop arrived as an interim 1986 model and all 1986 convertibles sold to the public were designated as pace car replicas. The actual Indy pace car was yellow, a new Corvette color for 1986, but the replicas could be any solid Corvette exterior color.

Anti-lock braking also arrived with the 1986 Corvette model. An adaptation of Bosch's system, the Corvette's ABS employed rotational speed sensors at each wheel to feed data to a computerized Electronic Control Unit. Brake line pressure was then automatically distributed under panic stop situations for optimum braking without wheel lockup and loss of steering control.

There were no engine choices during the 1984-86 period, but there were engine refinements each year. The 1984 engine was a carryover of the 1982's 350-cubic-inch V-8 with cross-fire injection. Despite the name, the fuel delivery

1987 Corvette Convertible. Chevrolet photo.

1986 Corvette Colors/Options

Color Code	Body Color	Soft Top Color
13	Silver	Black/White
18	Medium Gray	Black/White
20	Medium Blue	Black/White
35	Yellow	Black/White
40	White	Black/White/Saddle
41	Black	Black/White/Saddle
53	Gold	Black/Saddle
59	Silver Beige	Black
69	Medium Brown	Saddle
74	Dark Red	Black/White/Saddle
81	Bright Red	Black/White/Saddle
13/18	Silver/Gray	n/a
18/41	Gray/Black	n/a
40/13	White/Silver	n/a
59/69	Silver Beige/Brown	n/a

INTERIOR COLORS: Graphite, Medium Gray, Blue, Saddle, Bronze, Red

Order #	Item Description	Sticker Price
1YY07	Corvette Sport Coupe	27,502.00
1YY67	Corvette Convertible	32,507.00
A—2	Leather Seats	400.00
A—8	Sport Seats, Leather	1,025.00
AG9	Power Driver Seat	225.00
B4P	Radiator Boost Fan	75.00
C2L	Dual Removable Roof Panels	895.00
24S	Removable Roof Panel—Blue Tint	595.00
64S	Removable Roof Panel—Bronze Tint	595.00
C68	Electronic Air Conditioning Control	150.00
D84	Two-Tone Paint	428.00
FG3	Delco-Bilstein Shock Absorbers	189.00
G92	Performance Axle Ratio	22.00
KC4	Engine Oil Cooler	110.00
K34	Cruise Control	185.00
MM4	4-Speed Transmission	n/c
MX0	Automatic Transmission	n/c
NN5	California Emissions	99.00
UL5	Radio Delete	256.00
UM6	Electronically Tuned Stereo/Cassette	122.00
UU8	Delco-Bose Stereo System	895.00
VO1	Heavy-Duty Radiator	40.00
Z51	Performance Handling Package	470.00
Z6A	Defogger System	165.00

1987 Corvette Colors/Options

Color Code	Body Color	Soft Top Color
13	Silver	Black/White
18	Medium Gray	Black/White
20	Medium Blue	Black/White
35	Yellow	Black/White
40	White	Black/White/Saddle
41	Black	Black/White/Saddle
53	Gold	Black/Saddle
59	Silver Beige	Black
66	Copper	Black/Saddle
69	Medium Brown	Saddle
74	Dark Red	Black/White/Saddle
81	Bright Red	Black/White/Saddle
13/18	Silver/Gray	n/a
18/41	Gray/Black	n/a
40/13	White/Silver	n/a
59/69	Silver Beige/Brown	n/a

INTERIOR COLORS: Graphite, Medium Gray, Blue, Saddle, Bronze, Red

Order #	Item Description	Sticker Price
1YY07	Corvette Sport Coupe	28,474.00
1YY67	Corvette Convertible	33,647.00
A—2	Leather Seats	400.00
A—8	Sport Seats, Leather	1,025.00
AC1	Power Passenger Seat	240.00
AC3	Power Driver Seat	240.00
B2K	Callaway Twin Turbo Engine	19,995.00
B4P	Radiator Boost Fan	75.00
C2L	Dual Removable Roof Panels	915.00
24S	Removable Roof Panel—Blue Tint	615.00
64S	Removable Roof Panel—Bronze Tint	615.00
C68	Electronic Air Conditioning Control	150.00
DL8	Twin Remote Heated Mirrors	38.00
D74	Illuminated Driver Vanity Mirror	58.00
D84	Two-Tone Paint	428.00
FG3	Delco-Bilstein Shock Absorbers	189.00
G92	Performance Axle Ratio	22.00
KC4	Engine Oil Cooler	110.00
K34	Cruise Control	185.00
MM4	4-Speed Transmission	n/c
MX0	Automatic Transmission	n/c
NN5	California Emissions	99.00
UJ6	Low Tire Pressure Indicator	325.00
UL5	Radio Delete	256.00
UM6	Electronically Tuned Stereo/Cassette	132.00
UU8	Delco-Bose Stereo System	905.00
VO1	Heavy-Duty Radiator	40.00
Z51	Performance Handling Package	795.00
Z52	Sport Handling Package	470.00
Z6A	Defogger System	165.00

system was more carburetion than fuel injection. Real fuel injection came in 1985 with the debut of Corvette's tuned-port injection, a nifty change of hardware that yielded an increase from 205 horsepower to 230, and ten percent better fuel economy. Aluminum heads were included with 1986 models, but not during the first months of production (all convertibles *did* get aluminum heads). In addition to weight savings, the aluminum heads had a more efficient design that added another five horsepower.

For 1987, roller valve lifters were added to reduce internal friction in the standard Corvette engine, yielding five more horsepower than 1986's aluminum-head motor. For high rollers, Corvette engineers cooperated with Callaway Engineering to develop a 345-horsepower twin-turbo Corvette capable of 0-60 mph in 4.6 seconds and a top speed of 175 mph. Chevrolet shipped completed Corvettes to Callaway's shop in Old Lyme, Connecticut, where the engines were swapped for new units rebuilt by Callaway. Chevy dealers could order these ferocious machines by specifying RPO B2K. Additionally, Callaway Twin Turbos had street-legal emissions and the standard Corvette warranty. The option cost for the package was a cool $19,995.00.

Corvettes built between 1984 and 1987 may look similar, but there's a lot to consider before purchase. Suspension, transmission, seat materials—all have to be weighed. There weren't engine choices during any of these model years, except for the expensive Callaway Twin Turbo in 1987, but improvements to the standard engine year to year were significant.

When these cars populated used car lots, the big value break was between 1985 and 1986, with the earlier years thought to be less desirable. It was due to addition of ABS braking in 1986, but the major refinements (softer springs and fuel injection) came in 1985, so it is an underpriced value. There are also great bargains in 1984 models, especially late-production cars with base suspensions. The 1984 with Z51 suspension was really too brutal for everyday use, but I'll give you the another perspective on that conclusion. At a media event in 1993, I asked a Chevy engineer which Corvette suspension was his favorite. He surprised me by picking the 1984 Z51. His rationale was that he could live with the harshness to get a car with the ultimate in handling.

No question that 1986 and 1987 models were the most refined of this group. Except for early 1986 coupes, all had aluminum heads. The 240-horsepower, roller-lifter engine of the 1987 made it the most powerful since 1974 (excluding the Callaway), and 1987's RPO Z52 option was the best overall suspension of the 1984-1987 period for spirited street use.

Bringing a convertible back to the Corvette lineup in 1986 required a lot more than just removing the roof. In this display, the pieces painted white were those added to stiffen the chassis. Author photo.

CHAPTER 15
1988-1990 CORVETTE

✪✪✪
✪✪✪((35th Anniversary)
✪✪✪✪ (ZR-1, Callaway)
✪✪✪✪✪ (Challenge Racers)

Serial Nos. 1988: 1G1YY2186J5100001-1G1YY2186J5122789
          1989: 1G1YY2186K5100001-1G1YY2186K5126412
          1990: 1G1YY2380L5100001-1G1YY2380L5120597
          1990: 1G1YZ23J6L5800001-1G1YZ23J6L5803049 (ZR-1)
          (For convertibles, sixth digit is a 3)
          (ninth digit is a check digit and varies)

By 1990, the Corvette was into its seventh year using the body/chassis design that made its debut as a 1984 model. With the Japanese churning out all-new cars in four-year product cycles during the period, one might have expected the Corvette's appeal to be running on empty. Instead, *no* other vehicle on earth garnered more media attention in the decade's last two years than Chevrolet's two-seater.

Credit most of this to the ZR-1 (RPO ZR1). The media got wind of it by 1988 and tagged it "King of the Hill," a title Chevrolet didn't like and disclaimed. When it finally arrived as a 1990 model option, the ZR-1 name needed no additional embellishments. Its heartbeat was supplied by a completely new, all-aluminum, thirty-two valve engine. The 1984 model put the Corvette in the big leagues, but the 1990 ZR-1 gave it superstar status. Except for a Ferrari F40, a race car dressed in street clothes with a price in the stars, nothing on the street, but nothing, could outperform the ZR-1.

More on this and 1990's other big claim to fame, its new interior, in a moment. First, let's backtrack because while 1990 was a milestone year, the stage was set by the 1988 and 1989 models.

The three years were linked by a new wheel design. Actually, two wheels were used in 1988. The standard wheel had six slots; a variation had twelve and came with RPO Z51 and Z52 options. For 1989 and 1990, the twelve slot wheel was standard with all models. Dealer brochures called 1990's wheels "new and lighter," but it was a small revision that left the center trim cap off and the lug nuts exposed.

Engineers changed spring rates several times in previous years as they refined Corvette suspensions, but these were established and not changed during 1988-1990. However, 1988 did see significant front suspension revisions to achieve zero scrub radius, and to reduce steering wheel fight from brake torque and road inputs.

Speaking of brakes, 1988 Corvettes got new dual-piston front brakes and a new-design rear emergency brake which activated the pads instead of small, separate emergency drum brakes as in all previous disk-brake Corvettes.

If it sounds like Chevrolet wouldn't leave well enough alone, it's true. Why improve brakes that were already tremendous? The impetus was racing, specifically SCCA (Sport Car Club of America) Pro Showroom Stock, a series started in 1985. Unlike amateur Showroom Stock races, which were short

148

No doubt about it, Corvettes were the hot topic of conversation again in 1990 thanks to the debut of RPO ZR1, a $27,016 option that included unique body panels from the doors rearward and a brand-new 32-valve powerplant designed jointly by Chevrolet and Lotus. **Chevrolet photos.**

Chevrolet celebrated thirty-five years of Corvette production with this handsome anniversary edition (coupes only). Chevrolet photo.

1988 Corvette Colors/Options

Color Code	Body Color	Soft Top Color
13	Silver	Black/White
20	Medium Blue	Black/White
28	Dark Blue	Black/White/Saddle
35	Yellow	Black/White
40	White	Black/White/Saddle
41	Black	Black/White/Saddle
74	Dark Red	Black/White/Saddle
81	Bright Red	Black/White/Saddle
90	Gray	Black/White
96	Charcoal	Black/White/Saddle
40/41	White/Black	n/a

INTERIOR COLORS: Black, Grey, Red, Saddle, Blue.

Order	Item Description	Sticker Price
1YY07	Corvette Sport Coupe	29,995.00
1YY67	Corvette Convertible	35,295.00
A—2	Leather Seats	400.00
A—8	Sport Seats, Leather	1,025.00
AC1	Power Passenger Seat	240.00
AC3	Power Driver Seat	240.00
B2K	Callaway Twin Turbo Engine	26,345.00
B4P	Radiator Boost Fan	75.00
C2L	Dual Removable Roof Panels	915.00
24S	Removable Roof Panel—Blue Tint	615.00
64S	Removable Roof Panel—Bronze Tint	615.00
C68	Electronic Air Conditioning Control	150.00
DL8	Twin Remote Heated Mirrors	35.00
D74	Illuminated Driver Vanity Mirror	58.00
FG3	Delco-Bilstein Shock Absorbers	189.00
G92	Performance Axle Ratio	22.00
KC4	Engine Oil Cooler	110.00
MM4	4-Speed Transmission	n/c
MX0	Automatic Transmission	n/c
NN5	California Emissions	99.00
UL5	Radio Delete	-297.00
UU8	Delco-Bose Stereo System	773.00
V01	Heavy-Duty Radiator	40.00
Z01	35th Special Edition Package	4,795.00
Z51	Performance Handling Package	1,295.00
Z52	Sport Handling Package	970.00
Z6A	Defogger System	165.00

1989 Corvette Colors/Options

Color Code	Body Color	Soft Top Color
10	White	Black/White/Saddle
20	Medium Blue	Black/White
28	Dark Blue	Black/White/Saddle
41	Black	Black/White/Saddle
68	Dark Red	Black/White/Saddle
81	Bright Red	Black/White/Saddle
90	Grey	Black/White
96	Charcoal	Black/White/Saddle

INTERIOR COLORS: Black, Grey, Red, Saddle, Blue.

Order	Item Description	Sticker Price
1YY07	Corvette Sport Coupe	$32,045.00
1YY67	Corvette Convertible	37,285.00
CVAB	Coupe Base Group	n/c
CVAB	Coupe Base Group w/RPO UU8	773.00
CVA1	Coupe Group 1 (RPO C68, UU8, AC3)	1,163.00
CYAB	Conv Base Group	n/c
CYAB	Conv Base Group w/RPO UU8	773.00
CYA1	Conv Group 1 (RPO C68, UU8, AC3)	1,163.00
A—2	Leather Seats	400.00
A—8	Sport Seats, Leather	1,025.00
AC1	Power Passenger Seat	240.00
AC3	Power Driver Seat	240.00
B2K	Callaway Twin Turbo Engine	26,345.00
B4P	Radiator Boost Fan	75.00
CC2	Auxiliary Hardtop (conv)	1,995.00
C2L	Dual Removable Roof Panels	915.00
24S	Removable Roof Panel—Blue Tint	615.00
64S	Removable Roof Panel—Bronze Tint	615.00
C68	Electronic Air Conditioning Control	150.00
D74	Illuminated Driver Vanity Mirror	58.00
FX3	Selective Ride/Handling Package	1,695.00
G92	Performance Axle Ratio	22.00
K05	Engine Block Heater	20.00
KC4	Engine Oil Cooler	110.00
MN6	6-Speed Manual Transmission	n/c
MX0	Automatic Transmission	n/c
NN5	California Emissions	100.00
UJ6	Low Tire Pressure Indicator	325.00
UU8	Delco-Bose Stereo System	*
V01	Heavy-Duty Radiator	40.00
V56	Luggage Rack (conv)	140.00
Z51	Performance Handling Package	575.00

*See base option groups for pricing.

sprints lasting less than an hour, Pro Showroom Stock races were endurance events from four to twenty-four hours. In 1985, 1986, and 1987 seasons, Corvettes won every race. Other cars, most often Porsche 944 Turbos, kept up for a while, but couldn't last. Corvettes had to race in their own Corvette Challenge series in 1988 and 1989, because the competition couldn't cut it.

Corvette's racing durability was no accident. In the Corvette's first outing in 1985, things failed. Wheel studs broke, hubs cracked and ignition modules shorted. Chevrolet engineers contracted the racing team of Morrison & Cook to simulate races, six hours at first, then longer and longer, up to twenty-four hours. Engineers would analyze each failure along the way, make the necessary design changes, then move on.

These improvements went right into production Corvettes. Which years? Quoting Doug Robinson, the man who coordinated Chevy's racing program: "The 1986 was the first year where things from Showroom Stock racing began to benefit the production car. That year probably saw the most. In 1987, we added the power steering cooler to the Z51 purely because of racing. On the street, you'd never get it hot enough to cause a problem. But for racing, it was the last weak link. For 1988, we optimized the suspension geometry, and the new brake design was second to none compared to anything anyone's ever put on a street car."

Another weakness racing uncovered was the manual transmission. It seldom failed catastrophically in street use as it did in racing, but Chevy engineers went to a completely new design for the 1989 model (the same year they thought the ZR-1 would debut). The new unit was a six-speed designed jointly with ZF (Zahnradfabrik Friedrichshafen), and built by ZF in Germany. To help fuel economy in EPA tests, a computer sensed a non-performance situation and bypassed second and third gears by routing the shift lever to fourth from first. The parameters were restrictive enough, however, that this didn't happen too often in everyday driving.

The standard engine for 1988 and 1989 Corvettes continued to be the trusty 350-cubic-inch small-block rated at either 240 hp or 245 hp, the latter for coupes with 3.07:1 axle ratios. The extra 5 hp came from less restrictive mufflers, deemed too loud for convertibles and 2.59-axle coupes. For 1990, horsepower went to 245 and 250, thanks to a speed density control system and lighter pistons.

The Callaway Twin Turbo described in the previous chapter continued to be available all three years. It has been included in this book's option charts as RPO B2K, though it technically wasn't a Chevrolet option. When a Chevrolet dealer ordered RPO B2K, code SEO (Special Equipment Order) Z5G was triggered at Bowling Green. A Corvette thus earmarked received special build instructions and was shipped directly to Callaway's shop in Connecticut.

All this engine news paled by comparison to RPO LT5, the powerplant for the long-awaited ZR-1. Who hadn't heard of this new Corvette by the time of its official introduction as a 1990 model in September 1989? Yet, the story of the ZR-1 started much earlier. According to Jim Minneker, Corvette's powertrain manager, it began in May 1985 when Chevrolet contracted Lotus Engineering in England to develop new cylinder heads for the stock Corvette engine. By August 1985, Tony Rudd, Lotus's managing director, convinced Chevrolet an all-new motor was needed. The power expected of the new motor, something in the 400-hp range, led Chevrolet to expand the project to include a special wide-body rear to accept wider rubber. The first motor was running in May 1986, the first prototype car (of roughly one-hundred) in August 1986. According to Minneker, the real driving force behind the ZR-1 was a desire on the part of Chevrolet to showcase technology that they'd already developed but had been "hiding in the weeds."

Why Lotus? No, it was not GM's ownership of Lotus; that came later. Lotus was selected because Chevrolet respected their technical capabilities. As for going outside General Motors, the pain of the early eighties' auto recession taught auto companies to operate with lean professional staffs and go outside for special projects. Make no mistake about it. Chevrolet engineers worked hand-in-hand with Lotus in developing the LT5. All deserve credit.

The ZR-1 story is extensive enough to fill its own book (it has), but here's an overview of the content: The main component was the LT5 engine, a thirty-two-valve design with four overhead cams, aluminum heads, and aluminum block. The engine had the same 350-cubic-inch displacement, 90-degree V8 configuration and 4.4-inch bore spacing as the standard Corvette engine, but they shared virtually nothing except accessories. Assembly of engines was contracted to Mercury Marine in Stillwater, Oklahoma, but vehicles were assembled along with standard Corvettes in Bowling Green, Kentucky.

Available as manual-transmission coupes only, the ZR-1 body was an inch longer and three inches wider than a stock Corvette. The rear body facia flared out to accept Goodyear Z-rated P315/35ZR17 tires on eleven-inch rims, and this required different doors, rear quarters, rockers, rear facia, and rear upper panel. RPOs FX3 (Selective Ride Control), UJ6 (Low Pressure Warning), U1F (Delco-Bose CD), power driver and passenger seats, sport leather seats, and a specially coated "solar" windshield were included.

So much has been written about the ZR-1's extraordinary performance, it won't be repeated here. The real measure of Chevrolet's achievement was in the ZR-1's sophistication and reliability. It's one thing to drop a hot engine into a race chassis and turn big numbers. It's quite another to get the numbers in a civilized car that stays glued together. Chevrolet did it and at a price, it could be argued, that was downright reasonable.

The Selective Ride Control mentioned as standard with ZR-1 was optional with Z51 coupes in 1989, and with all other 1990s. Developed by Chevy and Bilstein Engineering, this feature allowed driver control over shock absorber damping via a three-position control switch on the console. Within each of the three modes, Touring, Sport, and Performance, there were six different shock absorber damping levels, dependent on vehicle speed.

ZR-1 got the headlines, but interior changes deserve mention, too. New seat designs arrived in 1989, then for 1990 the balance of the interior was redone. Cloth seats continued to be standard. Leather covering for the same seats was optional. Sport seats (leather only) were available only with Z51-equipped 1989s, then across the board for 1990.

"Driver oriented" properly described the theme for the new interior design as it enveloped the driver from door panel to console. Chevy called the instrument panel "hybrid" because it combined a digital speedometer with analog tachometer and secondary gauges. An airbag was added to the driver's side, a glovebox to the passenger's.

What does all this mean for a buyer? For starters, 1988, 1989, and 1990 were great Corvettes. The revised front suspension geometry made already good steering feel superb. The new wheel style came along in 1988, as did a thirty-fifth anniversary edition in white with black roof band, and white leather

1990 Corvette Colors/Options

Color Code	Body Color	Soft Top Color
10	White	Black/White/Saddle
25	Steel Blue	Black/White
41	Black	Black/White
42	Turquoise	Black/Saddle
53	Yellow	Black/White/Saddle
68	Dark Red	Black/White/Saddle
80	Quasar Blue	Black/Saddle
81	Bright Red	Black/White/Saddle
91	Polo Green	Black/Saddle
96	Charcoal	Black/Saddle

INTERIOR COLORS: Black, Grey, Red, Saddle, Blue.

Order	Item Description	Sticker Price
1YY07	Corvette Sport Coupe	32,479.00
1YY67	Corvette Convertible	37,764.00
CVAB	Coupe Base Group	n/c
CVAB	Coupe Base Group w/RPO UU8	823.00
CVAB	Coupe Base Group w/RPO U1F	1,219.00
CVA1	Coupe Group 1 (RPO C68, UU8, AC3)	1,273.00
CVA1	Coupe Group 1 (RPO C68, U1F, AC3)	1,669.00
CYAB	Conv Base Group	n/c
CYAB	Conv Base Group w/RPO UU8	823.00
CYAB	Conv Base Group w/RPO U1F	1,219.00
CYA1	Conv Group 1 (RPO C68, UU8, AC3)	1,273.00
CYA1	Conv Group 1 (RPO C68, U1F, AC3)	1,669.00
A—2	Leather Seats	425.00
A—8	Sport Seats, Leather	1,050.00
AC1	Power Passenger Seat	270.00
AC3	Power Driver Seat	270.00
B2K	Callaway Twin Turbo Engine	26,895.00
CC2	Auxiliary Hardtop (Conv)	1,995.00
C2L	Dual Removable Roof Panels	915.00
24S	Removable Roof Panel—Blue Tint	615.00
64S	Removable Roof Panel—Bronze Tint	615.00
C68	Electronic Air Conditioning Control	180.00
FX3	Selective Ride/Handling Package	1,695.00
G92	Performance Axle Ratio	22.00
K05	Engine Block Heater	20.00
KC4	Engine Oil Cooler	110.00
MN6	6-Speed Manual Transmission	n/c
MX0	Automatic Transmission	n/c
NN5	California Emissions	100.00
UJ6	Low Tire Pressure Indicator	325.00
UU8	Delco-Bose Stereo System	*
U1F	Delco-Bose Stereo System (w/CD)	*
V56	Luggage Rack (Conv)	140.00
Z51	Performance Handling Package	460.00
ZR1	Special Performance Package	27,016.00

*See base option groups for pricing.

Here's the most refined version of the Corvette's digital instrument panel (1989 shown above) and the new "hybrid" design for 1990 which combined a digital speedometer with analog tachometer and secondary instruments. The 1990 interior emphasized a driver-oriented approach, but increased the confined feel of the Corvette cockpit, particularly for the passenger. New features included a driver-side airbag and a passenger-side glovebox. Chevrolet photos.

The top photo shows a 1988 Corvette coupe with the standard six-slot wheels used only that year. The optional-for-1988 and standard wheel for 1989 and 1990 with twelve slots is shown on the convertible, along with the removable hardtop which hit the option list in 1989 at $1995.00. Although the LT-5 engines were assembled by Mercury Marine in Stillwater, Oklahoma, ZR-1 vehicles were built along with other Corvettes at the Bowling Green, Kentucky, plant. Chevrolet photos.

1986-1989-1990 Corvette

BASE ENGINE

Type: . . . . Chevrolet ohv V-8
Bore x stroke, inches: 4.00x3.48
Displacement, inches: 350
Compression ratio: 9.5:1
Carburetion: . . . . Multi-point fuel injection
Horsepower: . . 240 or 245 (1988, 1989), 245 or 250 (1990).
Distributor: . . . . High energy ignition
Other engines offered: For 1988 and 1989, only base engines were offered by Chevrolet, but the Callaway Twin Turbo engine option could be ordered through Chevrolet dealers for installation by Callaway Engineering. In 1990, option RPO ZR1 included the 32-valve, 350-cid, RPO LT5 engine.

CHASSIS AND DRIVETRAIN

Clutch: . . . . Single dry-plate (manual)
Transmissions: . . . . . . 4-speed automatic with overdrive and highstall torque converter; 4-speed manual with computer controlled overdrive (manual override) in 2nd, 3rd, and 4th gears (1988); 6-speed manual with computer controlled 1st to 4th gate (1989, 1990).

Front suspension: . . . Single transverse leaf spring, tube-type shock absorbers, upper and lower A-arms, stabilizer bar.

Rear suspension: . . . Single transverse leaf spring, tube-type shock absorbers, upper and lower control arms, stabilizer bar.

Frame: . . . . All-welded body-frame integral construction. Bolt-in front crossmember to allow bottom-loaded engine.

General:

Wheelbase, inches: 96.2
Track, front, inches: 59.6
        rear, inches: 60.4 (61.9 ZR-1)
Brakes: . . . . Disc, four-wheel
Tire Size: . . . . . . P255/50ZR16 (base 1988), P275/40ZR17 (opt 1988, base 1989-1990), P235/35ZR17 (1990 ZR-1).
Wheel material: . . . . Aluminum alloy
Wheel sizes, inches: 16x8.5, 16x9.5, 17x9.5
Body material: . . . . fiberglass
Assembly plant: . . . . Bowling Green, Kentucky

seats. If you like white, you'll love it. Production was relatively low at 2,050, so future appreciation for nice examples is a good bet.

I've owned two Corvettes with the 4+3 manual transmission last used in 1988. No repairs were required and I enjoyed these gearboxes. The six-speed manual of 1989 and later was a stronger unit, but it had the computer-aided first-to-fourth shift override that could be a nuisance. Overall, the six-speed *is* the better choice, especially for hard use, but don't rule out the 4+3.

The SCCA Corvette Challenge racing series created factory-built, streetable race cars. For 1988, the Corvette plant built fifty-six cars and Protofab Inc., in Wixom, Michigan, installed roll cages and other safety gear in fifty. Engines were stock, but matched for power and sealed. During the season, most engines were switched by Chevy for new engines, better matched for power.

In 1989, Bowling Green built sixty cars to Corvette Challenge specs. Higher-output engines were shipped from Chevy to Specialized Vehicles Inc., in Troy, Michigan, where they were equalized for power and sealed. Powell Development America in Wixom, Michigan, switched these special engines for the originals, and installed racing safety parts in thirty cars. At the end of the season, the original numbers-matching engines were returned to the racers.

Chevy dealers ordered twenty-three 1990 Corvettes destined for the new World Challenge race series. Merchandising code R9G triggered changes from normal build. Owners could buy racing engines from Chevrolet, or build their own. Race modifications were the owners' responsibility.

The 1988-89 Corvette Challenge models and the 1990 World Challenge models have special collector status. These were unusual programs, especially the sealed engines of 1988-89. Understanding the mentality of Corvette collectors, Chevrolet took special measures to build these cars for buyers who genuinely intended to race, so the quantities were quite low.

Back in the real world, all 1990 Corvettes had the new interior that most enthusiasts seem to favor. Personally, I prefer analog to digital, but Corvette's digital panels were very well done, whereas the 1990 hybrid wasn't. Neither interior had sufficient room, a problem aggravated by 1990's driver-isolated feel. The glovebox added in 1990 was a definite plus.

No three-year grouping of fourth-generation Corvettes offered more collector potential than 1988-1990. Callaway Twin-Turbos were available all three years. Special builds for the Corvette Challenge were sold in 1988 and 1989, then for World Challenge in 1990. ZR-1 arrived in 1990. Look beyond these special models at "stock" Corvettes and you'll find additional candidates worthy of consideration.

1988-89 Challenge cars were bona fide factory racers. Mike Yager photo.

CHAPTER 16
1991-1996 CORVETTE

✪✪✪
✪✪✪((Pace Car Replica)
✪✪✪✪ (Callaway, 1991-92 ZR-1)
✪✪✪✪✪ (1993-95 ZR-1)

Serial Nos. 1991: 1G1YY2386M5100001-1G1YY2386M5118595
1991: 1G1YZ23J6M5800001-1G1YZ23J6M5802044 (ZR-1)
1992: 1G1YY23P6N5100001-1G1YY23P6N5119955
1992: 1G1YZ23J6N5800001-1G1YZ23J6N5800502 (ZR-1)
1993: 1G1YY23PXP5100001-1G1YY23PXP5121142
1993: 1G1YZ23J3P5800001-1G1YZ23J3P5800448 (ZR-1)
1994: 1G1YY22P9R5100001-1G1YY22P9R5122882
1994: 1G1YZ22J9R5800001-1G1YZ22J9R5800448 (ZR-1)
1995: 1G1YY22P7S5100001-1G1YY22P7S5120294
1995: 1G1YZ22J0S5800001-1G1YZ22J0S5800448 (ZR-1)
1996: 1G1YY2257TP100001-1G1YY2251TP120536
1996: 1G1YY2251T5600001-1G1YY2251T5601000 (Grand Sport)
(For convertibles, sixth digit is a 3)
(In 1996, eighth digit is P for LT1, 5 for LT4)
(Ninth digit is a check digit and varies)

This chapter's inclusion of 1991 through 1996 model years should not suggest that little happened during this period, or that these models were the same. One visual feature that *does* unite this group is the new front-end design that arrived in 1991. It included wraparound front parking-cornering-fog lamps and went nicely with the new rear look introduced by the 1990 ZR-1, which was given to the rest of the lineup in 1991.

Remember, the ZR-1's larger rear wheels, tires, and track required wider bodywork from the doors rearward. For its 1990 debut, ZR-1's squared-off taillamps and convex rear facia made it stand out. Not so after 1991, because the rear of standard cars was redesigned to look like the ZR-1, even though the actual panels were not the same. Side by side from the rear, yes, you could spot the wider ZR-1. And, standard 1991-96 Corvettes had their high-mount stoplamps mounted in their rear facias, whereas all ZR-1 high-mount stoplamps were above the rear glass. But, jeez, considering the extra cost, ZR-1 owners felt they deserved a little more visual identity.

The philosophical dilemma was this: If two models are offered, one a high-priced premium unit, the other a standard unit, should the premium one have a unique look? Or should the models share appearance, so the prestige of the premium unit will boost appeal of the standard? Chevrolet chose the latter, saying in effect it cared most about sales of the higher-volume standard cars. Sales of the ZR-1 reflected this choice. From 1990's 3,049, the highest for any ZR-1 year, sales dropped to 2,044 in 1991. Sales continued south from there, for other reasons we'll examine in a moment.

A new wheel design appeared for 1991 and the styling of the wheels was

1991 Corvette convertible. Chevrolet photo.

1991 Corvette ZR-1. Chevrolet photo.

Appearance for 1992 mirrored 1991. Big 1992 news was the new, standard LT1 engine. With horsepower up to 300 (from 245 or 250), it made $31,683 extra for the 375-hp ZR-1 a much harder sell. LT1's Opti-Spark distributor (follow plug wires to front-of-engine location) required a 100% recall early in 1992 production. Chevrolet photos.

1991 Corvette Colors/Options

Color Code	Body Color	Soft Top Color
10	Arctic White	Black/Saddle/White
25	Steel Blue	Blue/Black/White
35	Yellow	Black/Saddle/White
41	Black	Black/Saddle/White
42	Turquoise	Blue/Black
75	Dark Red	Black/Saddle/White
80	Quasar Blue	Black/Saddle
81	Bright Red	Black/Saddle/White
91	Polo Green	Black/Saddle
96	Charcoal	Black/White

INTERIOR COLORS: Black, Blue, Red, Gray, Saddle

Order#	Item Description	Sticker Price
1YY07	Corvette Sport Coupe	32,455.00
1YY67	Corvette Convertible	38,770.00
AR9	Base Seats, Leather	425.00
AQ9	Sport Seats, Leather	1,050.00
AC1	Power Passenger Seat	290.00
AC3	Power Driver Seat	290.00
B2K	Callaway Twin Turbo Engine	33,000.00
CC2	Auxiliary Hardtop (convertible)	1,995.00
C2L	Dual Removable Roof Panels	915.00
24S	Removable Roof Panel–Blue Tint	615.00
64S	Removable Roof Panel–Bronze Tint	615.00
C68	Electronic Air Conditioning Control	180.00
FX3	Selective Ride/Handling Package	1,695.00
G92	Performance Axle Ratio	22.00
KC4	Engine Oil Cooler	110.00
MN6	6-Speed Manual Transmission	0.00
NN5	California Emissions	100.00
UJ6	Low Tire Pressure Warning Indicator	325.00
UU8	Delco-Bose Stereo System	823.00
U1F	Delco-Bose Stereo System (w/CD)	1,219.00
V56	Luggage Rack (convertible)	140.00
Z07	Adjustable Suspension Package (coupe)	2,155.00
ZR1	Special Performance Package	31,683.00

1992 Corvette Colors/Options

Color Code	Body Color	Soft Top Color
10	Arctic White	Blue/Beige/Black//White
35	Yellow	Beige/Black/White
41	Black	Beige/Black/White
43	Bright Aqua	Beige/Black/White
45	Polo Green II	Beige/Black/White
73	Black Rose	Beige/Black/White
75	Dark Red	Beige/Black/White
80	Quasar Blue	Beige/Black/White
81	Bright Red	Beige/Black/White

INTERIOR COLORS: Black, Light Beige, Light Gray, Red, White.

Order#	Item Description	Sticker Price
1YY07	Corvette Sport Coupe	33,635.00
1YY67	Corvette Convertible	40,145.00
AR9	Base Seats, Leather	475.00
AR9	Base Seats, White Leather	555.00
AQ9	Sport Seats, Leather	1,100.00
AQ9	Sport Seats, White Leather	1,180.00
AC1	Power Passenger Seat	305.00
AC3	Power Driver Seat	305.00
CC2	Auxiliary Hardtop (convertible)	1,995.00
C2L	Dual Removable Roof Panels	950.00
24S	Removable Roof Panel–Blue Tint	650.00
64S	Removable Roof Panel–Bronze Tint	650.00
C68	Electronic Air Conditioning Control	205.00
FX3	Selective Ride/Handling Package	1,695.00
G92	Performance Axle Ratio	50.00
MN6	6-Speed Manual Transmission	0.00
NN5	California Emissions	100.00
UJ6	Low Tire Pressure Warning Indicator	325.00
UU8	Delco-Bose Stereo System	823.00
U1F	Delco-Bose Stereo System (w/CD)	1,219.00
V56	Luggage Rack (convertible)	140.00
Z07	Adjustable Suspension Package (coupe)	2,045.00
ZR1	Special Performance Package	31,683.00

the same for all models, including ZR-1, even though wheel widths varied.

The Callaway Twin-Turbo package, not an actual Chevrolet-installed option but available through some Chevy dealers as RPO B4K, was last available in 1991. The end of this semiofficial Chevrolet liaison didn't stop Callaway from continuing to build specially modified Corvettes, though. In 1991, Callaway introduced its Speedster, with bodywork to die for. The following year, Callaway began the SuperNatural series, ZR-1's modified to produce 475 *naturally* aspirated horsepower.

In 1991, for the first time since 1984, the RPO Z51 performance handling package for coupes wasn't on the option list. But a new RPO Z07 *adjustable* suspension package was. Think of this as the FX3 selective ride and handling option combined with Z51 with a twist. Previously (1989-90), RPOs FX3 and Z51 could be combined, the result using some base suspension components so the adjustable range was from soft to firm. RPO Z07 used all heavy-duty suspension pieces so ride adjusted from firm to *very* firm. For those who do any competitive driving, this was a terrific package. For street-only, most would rate even the softest setting too harsh.

Corvette's 1991 base (and only) engine carried over with the same 245- or 250-horsepower ratings, depending on application.

Chevrolet built its one millionth Corvette during 1992, and two major improvements appeared this year. First, traction control was added as standard equipment. Called Acceleration Slip Regulation (ASR), the system was developed with Bosch (which also made Corvette's ABS) and engaged with the ignition, but could be turned off with an instrument panel switch. Engine spark retard, a throttle relaxer, and brake intervention were used to limit wheel spin when accelerating.

The second 1992 upgrade, also standard (except ZR-1), was the LT1 engine, a new-generation small block. Chevrolet worked some magic, staying with an iron block, two-valve per cylinder, pushrod design that increased horsepower to 300. The extra power came from computer-controlled ignition timing, low-restriction exhaust with twin converters, higher compression, revised camshaft, free-flow heads, and new multi-port fuel injection. Reverse cooling, where coolant went first to the heads *then* to the block was used to reduce ring friction and help cooling around the valve seats and spark plug bosses.

The new LT1 engine saw Chevy's first use of "Opti-Spark" ignition. An unusual distributor, with an internal rotating optical disc, mounted to the front of the engine, below the water pump. In its original production form, every Opti-Spark distributor was destined to fail. Chevrolet realized the extent of the problem, halted production, redesigned the distributor, then recalled every 1992 Corvette built. The recall was a model of how these things should be done. All's well now, but for history's sake, here's what happened.

Distributors are normally mounted high and dry. Engineers knew the Opti-Spark distributor's location might invite internal moisture formation. The trick was to provide a drain hole just large enough for venting. Special care was paid to this and engineers had the hole sized perfectly. In later validation testing, another group of engineers found that water could splash into the hole from below, so they wrote an engineering change making the drain hole smaller. Trouble was, this wasn't communicated to the original engineering group.

You guessed it. The distributors failed when internal condensation caused corrosion. The fix was nothing more than going back to the original size hole, but repositioning it so water couldn't splash in. How costly seemingly trivial errors can be.

If not giving ZR-1 models unique visual identity hurt sales, increasing output of the standard Corvette engine by fifty horsepower just about nailed the lid on the coffin. ZR-1 sales for 1992 dropped to 502, and rumors flew that it would be the last year. It wasn't, but sales never recovered.

Today, most agree that skipping the 1983 model year was a terrible mistake by Chevrolet, not just because it created a one year lineage gap, but it should have been Corvette's 30th year. When 1993 came along, Chevrolet wasn't about to let the 40th year pass quietly. A 40th Anniversary option, RPO Z25, was available across the board. It included Ruby Red metallic exterior, Ruby Red leather sport seats, power driver seat, special wheel trim and emblems. The option was a bargain at $1,455 but not rare as 6,749 sold.

To help justify its $31,683 option cost in light of the base Corvette's horsepower increase, 1993 ZR-1 models got an extra thirty horsepower (to 405), a result of cylinder-head and valvetrain work, and use of Mobil 1 synthetic oil.

In another first-for-GM, the 1993 Corvette introduced passive keyless entry. Working by proximity, a battery-operated key-fob transmitter sent a unique code picked up by a receiver in the car. It took no action by the owner. Approaching the vehicle unlocked it, turned on the interior light, and disarmed the theft deterrent. Walking away locked it and armed the alarm.

Cloth seats were still standard, but not common, in 1993 Corvettes. Of 21,590 cars sold, a mere 426 had cloth seats (all black). It was the last year for cloth; leather became standard the following year.

Big news for 1994 was the addition of a passenger-side airbag (and loss of glovebox). At the time, airbags were perceived as desirable and inclusion of

1991-1996 Corvette

BASE ENGINE (L98 1991, LT1 1992-1996)
Type: .... Chevrolet ohv V-8
Bore x Stroke, inches: 4.00x3.48
Displacement, inches: 350
Compression ratio: 10.0:1 (1991), 10.25:1 (1992)
    10.5:1 (1993-1995), 10.4:1 (1994).
Fuel Delivery: .... Multi-port fuel injection
Horsepower: 245 (1991), 300 (1992-1996)
Ignition: .... High energy ignition (1991)
    Opti-spark (1992-1996)
Other engines offered: .... From 1991 through 1996, RPO ZR1 included the 32-valve, 350-cid, LT5 engine (375-hp 1991-1992, 405-hp 1993-1995). In 1991, the Callaway Twin Turbo could be ordered through Chevrolet dealers. In 1996, the 330-hp RPO LT4 engine was optional, but required manual transmission.

CHASSIS AND DRIVETRAIN
Clutch: .... Single dry-plate (manual)
Transmissions: .... 4-speed automatic with overdrive and highstall torque converter; 6-speed manual with computer controlled 1st to 4th gate override.
Front suspension: .... Single transverse leaf spring, tube-type shock absorbers, upper and lower A-arms, stabilizer bar.

Rear suspension: .... Single transverse leaf spring, tube-type shock absorbers, upper and lower control arms, stabilizer bar.
Frame: .... All-welded body-frame integral construction. Bolt-in front crossmember for bottom-loaded engine.

General:
Wheelbase, inches: 96.2
Track, front, inches: 59.6 (1991), 57.7 (1992-1993) 57.5 (1994-1996)
Track, rear, inches: 60.4 (1991), 59.1 (1992-1996)
Brakes: .... Disc, four-wheel
Tire size, front: P275/40ZR17 (1991-1992) P255/45ZR17 (1993-1996)
Tire size, rear: P275/40ZR17 (1991-1992) P285/40ZR17 (1993-1996)
Wheel material: .... Aluminum alloy
Wheel size, front, inches: 17x9.5 (1991-1992) 17x8.5 (1993-1996)
Wheel size, rear, inches: 17x9.5
Body material: .... Fiberglass
Assembly plant: .... Bowling Green, Kentucky
ZR-1 specifics: All 1991-1995 ZR-1 models had 61.9" rear track, 17x11" rear wheels, and P315/35ZR17 rear tires. Front track was 59.6" with 17x9.5" wheels and P275/40ZR17 tires.

The 1993 ZR-1 coupe is shown at left above. Below is the standard 1993 coupe. The ZR-1 had unique, wider body panels from the doors rearward, and there were exterior identification clues. ZR-1 models had front fender emblems, high-mount stoplamps above the rear hatch instead of in the rear facia, and wider rear wheels. But it took a sharp and knowledgeable eye to detect these subtle differences. Sales of ZR-1 Corvettes fell well short of expectations partly because their visual impact didn't come close to matching firepower hidden under the hood, which for 1993 was boosted from 375 horsepower to 405. Chevrolet photos.

This 1993 interior shows optional sport leather seats. Control knobs for optional power assist for both seats are on the center console just behind the shift lever. Between the seat controls is the adjustment lever for the RPO FX3 Selective Ride and Handling suspension. Photo at left is the headrest embroidery for 1993 40th Anniversary models. These models had Ruby Red interiors and exteriors, including a Ruby Red soft top for convertibles, and special identification. Chevrolet photos.

dual systems helped sell any car with them. We know now that first-generation airbags had drawbacks. Children in child seats in front seats were vulnerable to the airbag itself, fatalities resulting from otherwise minor accidents. Safety advocates and manufacturers alike advised parents to place youngsters in rear seat locations. All well and good, except if you had more children than rear seats, or a sportscar with no rear seat at all.

The mess had its roots in airbag specs for the United States written with the misguided assumption that occupants wouldn't use seat belts. It was, "You're an idiot for not belting up, but we'll protect you anyway" mentality. Europeans wrote their standards assuming occupants *would* be held in position by seat belts. Our standards required bigger bags that deployed at roughly double the speed, nearly 200-mph! Something else. When airbags deploy, they do so loudly and with a shock wave due to the air that's being displaced within the cockpit. The smaller and better-sealed the compartment, the higher the potential for hearing damage. A second bag further aggravated the problem.

A nice feature of 1990-1993 Corvettes was the instrument panel glovebox. The original interior design for fourth-generation Corvettes (1984-1989) didn't have one, and for 1994-1996, the glovebox was replaced with a passenger-side airbag. Author photos.

1993 Corvette Colors/Options

Color Code	Body Color	Soft Top Color
10	Arctic White	Beige/Black/White
41	Black	Beige/Black/White
43	Bright Aqua	Beige/Black/White
45	Polo Green II	Beige/Black/White
53	Competition Yellow	Beige/Black/White
68	Ruby Red	Ruby Red
70	Torch Red	Beige/Black/White
73	Black Rose	Beige/Black/White
75	Dark Red	Beige/Black/White
80	Quasar Blue	Beige/Black/White

INTERIOR COLORS: Black, Light Beige, Light Gray, Red, Ruby Red, White.

Order#	Item Description	Sticker Price
1YY07	Corvette Sport Coupe	34,595.00
1YY67	Corvette Convertible	41,195.00
AR9	Base Seats, Leather	475.00
AR9	Base Seats, White Leather	555.00
AQ9	Sport Seats, Leather	1,100.00
AQ9	Sport Seats, White Leather	1,180.00
AC1	Power Passenger Seat	305.00
AC3	Power Driver Seat	305.00
CC2	Auxiliary Hardtop (convertible)	1,995.00
C2L	Dual Removable Roof Panels	950.00
24S	Removable Roof Panel–Blue Tint	650.00
64S	Removable Roof Panel–Bronze Tint	650.00
C68	Electronic Air Conditioning Control	205.00
FX3	Selective Ride/Handling Package	1,695.00
G92	Performance Axle Ratio	50.00
MN6	6-Speed Manual Transmission	0.00
NN5	California Emissions	100.00
UJ6	Low Tire Pressure Warning Indicator	325.00
UU8	Delco-Bose Stereo System	823.00
U1F	Delco-Bose Stereo System (w/CD)	1,219.00
V56	Luggage Rack (convertible)	140.00
Z07	Adjustable Suspension Package (coupe)	2,045.00
Z25	40th Anniversary Package	1,455.00
ZR1	Special Performance Package	31,683.00

The 1994 interior shows the analog/digital instrument displays, and the passenger-side airbag in place of the glovebox. Chevrolet photo.

Horsepower for ZR-1's LT5 started at 375 in 1990, then went to 405 in 1993 (photo above). The change came at midway in ZR-1's six-year life, but because production tailed off, just 1,344 of the 6,939 ZR-1s sold had the higher output engine. Author photo.

Here's the wheel used for 1994-1995 ZR-1s. This is a 1995, so it also had the new-style fender vents common to all 1995-1996 Corvettes. Author photo.

1994 Corvette Colors/Options

Color Code	Body Color	Soft Top Color
10	Arctic White	Beige/Black/White
28	Admiral Blue	Beige/Black/White
41	Black	Beige/Black/White
43	Bright Aqua	Beige/Black/White
45	Polo Green II	Beige/Black
53	Competition Yellow	Beige/Black/White
66	Copper	Beige/Black/White
70	Torch Red	Beige/Black/White
73	Black Rose	Beige/Black/White
75	Dark Red	Beige/Black/White

INTERIOR COLORS: Black, Light Beige, Light Gray, Red.

Order#	Item Description	Sticker Price
1YY07	Corvette Sport Coupe	34,595.00
1YY67	Corvette Convertible	41,195.00
AR9	Base Seats, Leather	475.00
AR9	Base Seats, White Leather	555.00
AQ9	Sport Seats, Leather	1,100.00
AQ9	Sport Seats, White Leather	1,180.00
AC1	Power Passenger Seat	305.00
AC3	Power Driver Seat	305.00
CC2	Auxiliary Hardtop (convertible)	1,995.00
C2L	Dual Removable Roof Panels	950.00
24S	Removable Roof Panel–Blue Tint	650.00
64S	Removable Roof Panel–Bronze Tint	650.00
C68	Electronic Air Conditioning Control	205.00
FX3	Selective Ride/Handling Package	1,695.00
G92	Performance Axle Ratio	50.00
MN6	6-Speed Manual Transmission	0.00
NN5	California Emissions	100.00
UJ6	Low Tire Pressure Warning Indicator	325.00
UU8	Delco-Bose Stereo System	823.00
U1F	Delco-Bose Stereo System (w/CD)	1,219.00
V56	Luggage Rack (convertible)	140.00
Z07	Adjustable Suspension Package (coupe)	2,045.00
Z25	40th Anniversary Package	1,455.00
ZR1	Special Performance Package	31,683.00

1995 Corvette convertible. Chevrolet photo.

For 1996, the last of the fourth-generation Corvettes, Chevrolet sold two special models. Above is the Grand Sport. Available in coupe or convertible, it came with 1996's optional 330-hp LT4 engine and manual transmission. Just 1,000 of these Admiral Blue-with-white-trim beauties were sold. At right is the Sebring Silver Collector Edition. Production was 5,412, but these were available with different options so lots of desirable combinations were possible. Both special models used ZR-1 style wheels, painted silver for Collector Editions, black for the Grand Sports. Chevrolet photos.

Advocates pointed out that benefits outweighed dangers. I've read that belted in, a driver-side airbag improves survival odds by 4%. I guess 4% is not nothing, but personally I'd prefer better restraints—wider belts and more secure anchoring—and a refund for airbags not installed. But that wasn't an available choice. As you consider which of the Corvette models in the 1991-1996 range meets your needs, factor in your life-style, your passengers, and what actions current law permits.

Enough of that. Another 1994 first was the switch to R-134A air-conditioning refrigerant, a non-ozone-depleting CFC substitute. R-134A has smaller molecules and is tougher to seal, requiring a thoroughly reworked system. It doesn't cool quite as well, but its future supply is assured.

ZR-1 models for 1994 finally had a unique wheel design, five-spoke beauties that fit the car's personality perfectly.

Goodyear's Extended Mobility Tires (EMTs) were a new option for 1994. "Run flat" bead construction permitted temporary use with little or no air. The low tire pressure warning option (RPO UJ6) was required so a driver would know if pressure was low. Running underinflated for fifty miles could damage an EMT, but actual driving range was much further. EMTs played a major role in the design of the fifth-generation 1997 Corvettes, but in 1994 they didn't make too big a splash as 2,781 were ordered at $70 per set.

For 1995, Corvette again paced the Indy 500. The race was noteworthy as the last before the big split caused by the formation of the Indianapolis Racing League. The car was noteworthy as just 527 replicas were sold. These were all convertibles with special Dark Purple and Arctic White exterior paint, white convertible tops, special graphics and trim.

Production of the ZR-1 ceased with the 1995 model year. Production of ZR1's LT5 engines by Mercury Marine in Oklahoma actually ended in November 1993. Chevrolet predetermined it would build 448 ZR-1s for each 1993, 1994, and 1995 model run. Tooling used by Mercury Marine was owned by GM, and was removed by the end of 1993. The specially sealed and packaged engines were shipped to Bowling Green for storage until needed. Mercury Marine had been responsible for some LT5 warranty repair, but after January 1, 1994, all service was handled by Chevrolet.

All knew 1996 would end the Corvette's fourth-generation. To maintain interest and sales, Chevrolet offered special models and an optional engine.

The engine was RPO LT4. Exclusive to Corvette, with 330 horsepower (30 more than the LT1), LT4 had higher compression, new head design, Crane roller rocker arms, revised camshaft, and other massaging. It was mated exclusively to six-speed manual transmissions. The base LT1, on the other hand, came only with a four-speed automatic. The LT4 engine was a stand-alone option at $1,450.

RPO Z15, the Collectors Edition, cost $1,250 and included Sebring Silver paint with special trim. Wheels duplicated the 1994-95 ZR-1 style but were painted silver. Red, black, or light gray interiors could be ordered, but soft tops for convertibles had to be black. Although a hefty 5,412 Collector Editions were sold, there was a lot of variety within that number. These could be coupe or convertible, base or optional engine, with any number of different option combinations.

The high-demand model for 1996 was the Grand Sport, RPO Z16. It included the LT4 engine, and therefore came only with six-speed manual. Paint was Admiral Blue with white center stripe and special detailing. Grand Sports

Ever since the cooperative effort that enabled customers to order Callaway Twin-Turbo Corvettes through Chevrolet dealers (1987-1991), Reeves Callaway's company in Old Lyme, Connecticut, has taken the lead in aftermarket Corvette offerings. Callaway called this spectacular rebodied convertible the "Speedster." Callaway photo.

1995 Corvette Colors/Options

Color Code	Body Color	Soft Top Color
05	Dark Purple	Beige/Black/White
05/10	Dark Purple/White	White
10	Arctic White	Beige/Black/White
28	Admiral Blue	Beige/Black/White
41	Black	Beige/Black/White
43	Bright Aqua	Beige/Black/White
45	Polo Green	Beige/Black
53	Competition Yellow	Beige/Black/White
70	Torch Red	Beige/Black/White
75	Dark Red	Beige/Black/White

INTERIOR COLORS: Black, Light Beige, Light Gray, Red.

Order#	Item Description	Sticker Price
1YY07	Corvette Sport Coupe	36,785.00
1YY67	Corvette Convertible	43,665.00
AG1	Power Driver Seat	305.00
AG2	Power Passenger Seat	305.00
AQ9	Sport Seats	625.00
CC2	Auxiliary Hardtop (convertible)	1,995.00
C2L	Dual Removable Roof Panels	950.00
24S	Removable Roof Panel–Blue Tint	650.00
64S	Removable Roof Panel–Bronze Tint	650.00
FX3	Selective Ride/Handling Package	1,695.00
G92	Performance Axle Ratio	50.00
MN6	6-Speed Manual Transmission	0.00
NG1	New York Emissions	100.00
N84	Spare Tire Delete	-100.00
UJ6	Low Tire Pressure Warning Indicator	325.00
U1F	Delco-Bose Stereo System (w/CD)	396.00
WY5	Extended Mobility Tires	70.00
YF5	California Emissions	100.00
Z07	Adjustable Suspension Package (coupe)	2,045.00
Z4Z	Indy 500 Pace Car Replica	2,816.00
ZR1	Special Performance Package	31,258.00

1996 Corvette Colors/Options

Color Code	Body Color	Soft Top Color
05	Dark Purple	Beige/Black/White
10	Arctic White	Beige/Black/White
13	Sebring Silver	Black
28	Admiral Blue	White
41	Black	Beige/Black/White
43	Bright Aqua	Beige/Black/White
45	Polo Green	Beige/Black
53	Competition Yellow	Beige/Black/White
70	Torch Red	Beige/Black/White

INTERIOR COLORS: Black, Light Beige, Light Gray, Red, Red & Black.

Order#	Item Description	Sticker Price
1YY07	Corvette Sport Coupe	37,225.00
1YY67	Corvette Convertible	45,060.00
AG1	Power Driver Seat	305.00
AG2	Power Passenger Seat	305.00
AQ9	Sport Seats	625.00
CC2	Auxiliary Hardtop (convertible)	1,995.00
C2L	Dual Removable Roof Panels	950.00
24S	Removable Roof Panel–Blue Tint	650.00
64S	Removable Roof Panel–Bronze Tint	650.00
F45	Selective Real Time Damping, electronic	1,695.00
G92	Performance Axle Ratio	50.00
LT4	350-cid, 330-hp Engine	1,450.00
MN6	6-Speed Manual Transmission	0.00
N84	Spare Tire Delete	-100.00
UJ6	Low Tire Pressure Warning Indicator	325.00
U1F	Delco-Bose Stereo System (w/CD)	396.00
WY5	Extended Mobility Tires	70.00
Z15	Collectors Edition	1,250.00
Z16	Grand Sport ($2,880 w/convertible)	3,250.00
Z51	Performance Handling Package	350.00

also used ZR-1 style wheels, but painted black, and with additional twists. Coupes had 11-inch wide rear wheels and rear fender flares. Grand Sport convertibles had 9.5-inch rear wheels and no rear fender flares. Grand Sport availability was limited, in part due to application problems with the white exterior graphics. Just 1,000 were sold. Like ZR-1s, Grand Sports had their own separate serial number sequencing.

It was pointed out earlier that RPO Z51 (Performance Handling Package) was discontinued in 1991. It returned in 1996 restricted, as before, to coupes.

Chevrolet efforts to maintain appeal of the fourth-generation paid off. Competitors folded their tents left and right, but Corvette sales stayed over twenty-thousand each of the 1991-1996 model years. *AutoWeek* presented results of an annual reader survey in its July 1, 1996 issue. Corvette won, with Viper second. Quoting *AutoWeek*, "With Chevrolet getting ready to roll out an all-new Corvette for the 1997 model year, *AutoWeek* readers find little fault with the current car, and they have returned it to the No. 1 position in their annual rating of the 10 American cars in which they have the most pride."

Read between the lines to pick the 1991-1996 model best suited to your needs. Think of these as used cars, not collector cars. After all, between 1991 and 1996, Chevrolet sold 128,316 Corvettes. But if the potential for future appreciation is a high priority, certainly ZR-1s come to mind. I especially like the prospects for 1994 and 1995 ZR-1s because of their low production, higher horsepower, and gutsy five-spoke wheel design. If you go this route, you *must* join the *ZR-1 Registry* (29 Lucille Dr, Sayville, NY, 11782), a well-organized, 2,400-member group complete with a top-notch newsletter. The nature of this car's LT5's engine construction conjures up possible future maintenance issues, but the power of the *Registry* to keep Chevrolet's attention and to share data with its members tempers concerns considerably.

Grand Sports had instant collector glow due to their low production stats, performance content, and last-of-the-generation status. The 1996 Collector Edition wasn't scarce, but some option combinations could be. The same could be said for 1993's anniversary package. The 1995 pace car replica *was* scarce, but with definite love-it or hate-it looks.

The Callaway Twin Turbo was last available through Chevy dealers in 1991. Historically, collectors have tended to shy away from anything without genuine Chevy linkage, but there was linkage with the Twin Turbos, and later Callaway Corvette efforts like the Speedster and the SuperNatural had so much raw appeal that surely some will be mega-dollar pieces.

In affirmation of the Corvette's unique cultural status, two Corvette museums opened during the 1991-1996 period. In 1992, Dr. Allen Schery opened the private *Corvette Hall of Fame and Americana Musuem* in Cooperstown, New York. Then in 1994, the *National Corvette Museum,* under the direction of the museum's foundation president Dan Gale, opened near the Corvette assembly plant in Bowling Green, Kentucky.

From 1991 through 1996 Chevrolet offered up a wonderful menu of Corvettes from which to select. Enthusiasts continued to rate these Corvettes high on their wish lists in magazine surveys. Customers perceived these models to be great performance values at their sticker prices, so just think of the steals many represent as *depreciated* used cars.

Serial Nos. 1997: 1G1YY22G1V5100001-1G1YY22G1V51-----

Five years after the introduction of the 1984 model, Chevrolet began laying the groundwork for another all-new Corvette. In 1989 surveys, customers ranked performance at the top of their Corvette wish list, no surprise, but build quality had climbed from nowhere to second place. Surveyed two years later, customers elevated quality to the most important attribute a new Corvette *must* have. This was due in part to demographics. Average household income for a new-Corvette buyer had reached six figures, and two-thirds were college educated. Performance, style, comfort, value . . . all were still important. But customers were making it clear that if a new Corvette didn't put it all together in a high-quality package, they weren't buying.

Specific to the fourth-generation 1984-1996 models, customers told Chevrolet they thought the ride was too harsh. It rattled. They didn't like the high step-over to get in. Once in, they didn't like the cramped cockpit, especially the narrow footwells. The Corvette has always been a pretty big car for a two-seater, yet its exterior dimensions weren't reflected in cockpit or luggage room. And despite providing reams of data, fourth-generation Corvette instrument displays were a constant source of criticism.

Chevrolet listened and planned a new Corvette to meet its customers' expectations for 1993 introduction. Starting in 1989, however, General Motors began losing huge sums of money and new-car programs were postponed or cancelled outright. The Corvette's planned introduction slid to 1994, then 1995, then went on indefinite hold. The new Corvette program was actually killed in 1992, but revived when executives reviewed proposals for the all-new Corvette. They realized that engineers and designers had dreamed up something very special.

The Corvette team came up with engineering solutions to customer demands. Instead of a "bird cage" frame with a center passenger cell and front and rear sub-assemblies, the 1997 got full-length "hydroformed" frame rails, the heart of a much stiffer structure. The advantages of hydroforming this huge structural member were precise shape control and elimination of multiple stampings (fourteen in the previous Corvette) and the welding operations associated with them.

The rigid structure reduced the side sill stepover by nearly four inches. But combining the transmission with the rear axle in the 1997 was the decision that really opened up interior space. Other changes helped too. The wheelbase increased a whopping 8.3 inches, from 96.2 to 104.5 inches. Yet overall length increased by barely an inch. Track increased 4.4 inches in the front and 2.9 in the rear (equal to the ZR-1).

In a nutshell, here's what Chevy engineers did. They designed a new chassis from scratch that was very rigid. They moved the wheels toward the

1997 Corvette. Chevrolet photos

Chevrolet called 1997's instrument panel "the end result of a 13-year evolution . . . good balance of utility and amenity." Digital (Driver Information Center) and analog displays were used, each where it "made the most sense." Ultraviolet (black) lighting illuminated the instruments, and cockpit room was much improved, especially in the footwells. Chevrolet photo.

1997's structure was built around a full-length perimeter frame with side rails manufactured from seamless tubular steel. The rails were "hydroformed" by a special high-pressure hydraulic press developed by GM. The rails were joined at their ends by welded-on bumper beams. Since the transmission was moved to the rear, the wide forward structural flaring normally required wasn't. The tunnel was closed off on the bottom by a plate attached with 36 bolts to further increase solidity. The floor was aircraft-style composite, in Corvette's case a sandwich of fiberglass above and below with balsa wood between. Chevrolet said the balsa made the floor 10 times stiffer than with composites alone. Lots of space-age synthetics were tried, but nothing beat good old balsa for the combination of stiffness, light weight, and damping performance. Chevrolet photos.

corners of the car. They relocated the transmission to the rear. The result was a better riding, better handling, far more comfortable vehicle. The best of all worlds. And they did all this while at the same time eliminating 34% of the vehicle's total parts. Was that a lot? About 1,500 pieces. That's a lot.

The last point is important. I was a GM student-employee in 1967 when *GM Mark of Excellence* stickers were attached to door jambs to signal a new quality emphasis. Trouble was, we still built the cars the same way. GM, like its competitors, realizes now that quality can be, to a degree, designed into an automobile. The rigid structure of the 1997 Corvette provided a firmer base for everything mounted to it, so shakes and rattles were minimized. And as Rod Michaelson, Corvette's Quality Engineering Manager, put it, "The 1,500 parts eliminated equates to 1,500 opportunities for something to go wrong that aren't there any more."

The 1997 was the most thoroughly "all new" model in Corvette history and that included the powerplant. The "LS1" engine, exclusive to Corvette in 1997, retained the 350-cubic-inch displacement and 4.4-inch bore centers of its predecessor, but otherwise was start-from-scratch and state-of-the-art in pushrod V8 design. The block was closed-deck aluminum alloy with cast-in cylinder liners. It had a deep skirt that extended past the main bearing caps, and a shallow cast-aluminum oil pan that was a structural member of the engine. At 345 horsepower and 350 lb-ft. torque, this engine required premium fuel and Mobil 1 synthetic oil, but didn't require major service until 100,000 miles. Electronic Throttle Control (ETC), or "fly by wire" eliminated a conventional mechanical accelerator linkage.

Designers wanted the 1997 to include styling cues that would link it to great Corvettes of the past. The rear kept the four-taillamp look that dated to 1961. The fender coves of 1956 through 1961 models were said to have inspired the 1997's sides. The exterior was a combination of smooth flowing shapes and a few hard edges, such as the lip defining the rear panel. Thank the wind tunnel, because engineers wanted all the benefits of a very slippery shape. When a car's speed doubles from 100-mph to 200-mph, drag quadruples. But you don't have to drive triple digit speeds, because lower drag means better fuel economy and stability in everyday driving. The 1997 Corvette's .29 coefficient of drag was the lowest of any GM car other than its electric. For comparison, the NSX cd was .332, the Porsche 911 Turbo .34, and the Toyota Supra Turbo .358. Corvettes of the past? Well, integrating the previously optional spoilers into the bumper caps in 1980 improved that Corvette's coefficient of drag from .503 to .443. Yes, we *have* come a long way, baby.

The 1997's best retro touch was the double-pod instrument panel that brought back memories of 1963-1967. A passenger grab bar was even included above the glovebox. Take a long look at it next time you're sitting in the passenger seat of this vehicle. Not only does it serve its obvious function, it is shaped to better aim the deployment of the airbag.

A large tachometer and speedometer took center stage in the instrument display, both flanked by secondary gauges, and illuminated by "black light" technology. Brake and clutch pedals were race-car style aluminum and, for the first time in Corvette's history, a real "dead pedal" was included. Finally.

The suspension used single composite leaf springs front and rear as before, but every piece of the 1997 suspension was new and unique to it. Fully independent, the suspension used short-long arm design at each corner. This

1997 Corvette Colors/Options

Color Code	Body Color
10	Arctic White
13	Sebring Silver Metallic
23	Nassau Blue Metallic
41	Black
53	Light Carmine Red Metallic
70	Torch Red
87	Fairway Green Metallic

INTERIOR COLORS: Black, Light Gray, Firethorn Red

Order	Item Description	Sticker Price
1YY07	Corvette Sport Coupe	37,495.00
AAB	Memory Package	150.00
AG2	Power Passenger Seat	305.00
AQ9	Sport Seats	625.00
B34	Floor Mats	25.00
B84	Body Side Moldings	75.00
CC3	Removable Roof Panel–blue tint	650.00
C2L	Dual Removable Roof Panels	950.00
CJ2	Dual Zone Air Conditioning	365.00
D42	Luggage Shade and Parcel Net	50.00
F45	Selective Real Time Damping, electronic	1,695.00
G92	Performance Axle Ratio	100.00
MN6	6-Speed Manual Transmission	815.00
NG1	Massachusetts/New York Emissions	170.00
T96	Fog Lamps	69.00
UN0	Stereo System with Compact Disc	100.00
U1S	Remote Compact Disc Changer	600.00
YF5	California Emissions	170.00
Z51	Performance Handling Package	350.00

The "LS1" engine for 1997 was just as new as the car. It was still a pushrod, two-valve-per-cylinder V8 in true Chevy small-block tradition, but was otherwise new and state-of-the art. Cylinder liners were cast into the aluminum block, and the block's skirts extended past the bearing caps. The long skirts dictated a shallow, cast-aluminum oil pan, designed with side oil reservoirs to keep oil available to the oil pump in hard cornering. Horsepower was 345, torque 350 lb-ft. David Kimble cutaway courtesy of Chevrolet.

1997 Corvette

BASE ENGINE (LS1)

Type: Chevrolet ohv V-8
Bore x Stroke, inches: 3.9x3.62
Displacement, inches: 350
Compression ratio: 10.1:1
Fuel Delivery: Sequential Fuel Injection
Horsepower: 345
Ignition: Coils near each spark plug, fired by crankshaft and camshaft position sensors.
Other engines offered: The LS1 was the only engine available in 1997 Corvettes and its use was restricted to Corvettes. A new design, the LS1's cylinder block was cast aluminum with cast-in cylinder liners.

CHASSIS AND DRIVETRAIN

Clutch: Single dry-plate (manual)
Transmissions: Rear-mounted 4-speed automatic with overdrive; rear-mounted six speed manual with computer-controlled 1st to 4th gate override.
Front Suspension: Single transverse-mounted composite leaf spring, monotube shock absorbers, short/long arm double wishbone suspension, forged-aluminum upper and lower control arms, stabilizer bar.
Rear Suspension: Single transverse-mounted composite leaf spring, monotube shock absorbers, short/long arm double wishbone suspension, cast-aluminum upper and lower control arms, stabilizer bar.
Frame: Perimeter with seamless, tubular steel side rails.

General:

Wheelbase, inches	104.5
Track, front, inches	62.0
rear, inches	62.1
Brakes:	Disc, four-wheel
Tire size, front	P245/45ZR17
Tire size, rear	P275/40ZR18
Wheel material:	Aluminum alloy
Wheel size, front, inches	17x8.5
Wheel size, rear, inches	18x9.5
Body material	Fiberglass
Assembly plant:	Bowling Green, Kentucky

geometry, also known as double wishbone or double A-arm, is common in race cars because of the control that can be dialed in. Wheel diameter remained 17-inch in front, but increased to 18-inch at the rear.

For improved luggage space and weight reduction, the 1997 was designed with no provision for a spare tire, tools, or jack, because Goodyear "extended mobility tires" (EMTs) were standard equipment. This was a bold decision not taken lightly. These tires run so well with no air pressure, most drivers wouldn't feel a problem. In as few as fifty miles, running with no air pressure can permanently damage an EMT, though the safe driving range is much further. The confidence to use these as standard issue and eliminate the spare was based first on a new high-performance design for the tire itself (EMTs had been optional since 1994), and second on a new low-tire pressure warning system. Low-tire pressure warning systems were previously optional too, but for 1997 the warning system was far more sophisticated.

Before, the low-tire pressure option consisted of transmitters strapped inside each wheel, which sensed pressure and triggered a receiver on the instrument panel to alert the driver to a low-pressure situation. But the display didn't tell which tire was low. The 1997 system used transmitters combined with the tire valves. With it, the driver was alerted not only if a tire dropped below 25 psi, but would be told *which* tire. Plus, the driver could call up an instrument panel readout to show the pressure of each tire, at any time, with accuracy to plus or minus one psi. Incredible.

More "user-friendly" is the right way to describe the 1997. The reachover to load into the storage area from the rear was reduced fourteen inches. Instead of unbolting the targa top with a wrench, the 1997's came off with three easy latches. The view out front allowed the driver to see an object in the road eighteen-feet closer than the previous generation.

Dave Hill, Corvette's Chief Engineer, said, "We examined our weak points and turned them into strengths. Things that were good, we made great. Things that were great, are now even better."

Simple words, but they convey one secret of Corvette's success. Always true to its mission, the Corvette has also been willing to stretch the envelope, to evolve so that it can continue to meet the expectations of its customers, the most loyal *and* most demanding bunch of car nuts on the planet.

Chevrolet photo

IDENTIFICATION NUMBERS

The VIN (vehicle identification number) is the most familiar number appearing on Corvettes. It is this number that appears on most titles (a few states have used engine numbers) and insurance policies.

A different VIN is assigned to each Corvette during assembly. Each car receives its number in sequence. The format of the number has changed over the years but the last digits always have indicated when a particular Corvette was assembled relative to others of the same year. For instance, the first 1953 Corvette VIN was E53F001001. The last was E53F001300, meaning total production for the year was 300. Note that you can determine the production quantities for each Corvette year in *Illustrated Corvette Buyer's Guide* by referring to the serial sequences at the head of each chapter. But one word of caution: Four thousand Corvette VIN tags disappeared during 1973 and these cars were never built. So while the 1973 sequence goes up to 34,464, only 30,464 were built. The missing numbers were 24,001 through 28,000.

The VIN is stamped into a plate that was attached to the body of each Corvette during manufacture. The location of the plate varies with different years. From 1953 through early 1960, the plate was attached to the driver's door post. All but early 1960 models and all 1961 and 1962 Corvettes had the plate attached to the steering column in the engine compartment. The 1963 through 1967 models had the plate attached to an instrument support brace visible below the glovebox. Starting with the 1968 models, federal law mandated that the VIN be visible through the windshield from outside the car on the driver's side; so the VIN plate of 1968 and newer Corvettes was located either on the windshield pillar or on top of the dash.

To aid in detecting stolen vehicles whose serial tags have been tampered with or switched, manufacturers also stamp the VIN into several locations on the frame. Enthusiasts often uncover these numbers during restorations and all Corvettes starting with the 1953 have them.

Starting in early 1960, the sequential portion of the VIN was stamped into the engine block on a pad just forward of the passenger-side cylinder head. Comparing the number stamped into the engine with the VIN serial tag thus enables the purchaser of a used Corvette to determine if its engine was originally installed by the factory. When Corvettes are advertised with the statement "numbers match," the match most often being referred to is that between the number stamped into the engine block and the VIN serial plate.

Unfortunately, the importance attached to engine originality by Corvette enthusiasts has led to the counterfeiting of Corvettes with engines that are not original. Since the sequential portion of the VIN was *stamped* into the engine block, the surface can be milled and restamped. But there are other numbers that can be checked.

One is the engine casting date code. This will be three or four characters—a letter followed by numbers. The letter indicates the month of casting. The day is indicated by the first one or two numbers. The last number indicates year. A date code of A122 translates to a block cast on January 12, 1962. Or 1972. Or 1982. The date code is on the top rear, passenger side of the block in Chevy small blocks. It's forward of the starter by the freeze plug on the passenger side of big blocks.

The beauty of the date code is that it is part of the block casting and protrudes rather than being stamped after casting. It is much more difficult to counterfeit. Attempts have been made by grinding off the original code, building up a weld bead, then reshaping a new number with a pencil grinder. Forgeries like this are rare and usually will not pass close inspection. For counterfeiting very desirable models, it is more common that a replacement block with an acceptable casting date is used.

The reason the engine casting date is important is that it obviously must precede the assembly of the Corvette itself. There is no exact time lag but typically something between a few days and two or three weeks pass between the time an engine block is cast and then installed in a new Corvette. There are reasons, rare but legitimate, that the time can be several months.

Determining a Corvette's originality is a process of elimination. As each questionable item is resolved, the likelihood of originality increases. But no one other than the original owner can ever be absolutely certain. As the stakes go higher, so do the rewards of counterfeiting. Certification by one of the major sanctioning groups, such as *Bloomington Gold* or the *National Corvette Restorers Society*, is certainly a plus.

Some enthusiasts just entering the market for a used Corvette are under the impression that they can obtain a copy of the original sales invoice or window sticker from Chevrolet. At this time, Chevrolet maintains it does not have the records. This is why original documentation is so prized.

Much of this is just good old common sense, but if you are at all uncomfortable about the authenticity of a Corvette you're considering, the best advice is to get knowledgeable assistance before making a costly mistake.

RECOMMENDED CORVETTE BOOKS

Scores of books have been written about Corvettes. Each has something of value, but some are more useful than others. Following are some personal favorites. This is far from a complete list, but if you digest the contents of these, you'll hold your own in any Corvette discussion.

Adams, Noland. *The Complete Corvette Restoration & Technical Guide*, Vol 1, 1953-1962. Kutztown, PA: Automobile Quarterly Publications. 1980.

Adams, Noland, and Paddock, Lowell. *The Complete Corvette Restoration & Technical Guide, Vol 2, 1963-1967*. Kutztown, PA: Automobile Quarterly Publications. 1988.

Antonick, Michael. *The Corvette Black Book*. Powell, OH; Michael Bruce Associates, Inc., 1978, 1980, 1983-1997.

Colvin, Alan L. *Chevrolet by the Numbers, 1965-69*. Cambridge, MA: Robert Bently, Inc. 1994.

Dobbins, M. F. *Vette Vues Fact Book of the 1963-1967 Sting Ray, 9th edition*. Hatboro, PA: Dr. M. F. Dobbins, 1989.

Dobbins, M. F. *Vette Vues Fact Book of the 1968-1972 Stingray. 4th edition*. Hatboro, PA: Dr. M. F. Dobbins, 1994.

Schefter, James. *All Corvettes Are Red*. New York, NY: Simon & Schuster, 1996.

Index